Praise for *Black*

"Intimate, wide-ranging, and sharply a
inspirational call for a more inclusive vision of Black community."

—***Publishers Weekly***

"Daniel Black takes his talent for writing about inexplicable pain and tells the stories of the marginalized. From police brutality to queer representation in the Black church, Daniel Black gives voice to experiences that show the remarkable resilience that has taken place, a collective celebration of fortitude and survival. A cultural criticism with stories that must be told."

—***She Reads***

"Black's new collection of essays dig deep into Blackness, history and racial tension in this country, while simultaneously serving as a powerful call to action and a celebration of Black culture."

—***NPR***

"*Black on Black* is a tour de force. Brilliant. Passionate. Deeply caring. One reads these essays and feels immediately enveloped in Daniel Black's love—even when he challenges you or when you might disagree. I really needed to read this book in these trying times."

—Eddie S. Glaude Jr., *New York Times* bestselling author of *Begin Again: James Baldwin's America and Its Urgent Lessons for Our Own*

"In a very real sense, the moral and ethical imperative of *Black on Black* is to speak a truth that renders black lives sacred, valued, and luminous. In this sense, like many of my generation, Daniel Black announces a prophetic lineage that places him among Baldwin's progeny, a fierce and passionate wish for the community, indeed the country, to heal and hold itself by standards that emerge from within rather than without, an unapologetic love that runs like fire beneath the history of skin. *Black on Black* is tender. Beautiful. Fierce beyond measure."

—Major Jackson, poet and author of *The Absurd Man*

"Daniel Black is one of our most treasured authors. *Black on Black* takes on a confessional mode, the stirring of a soul that shines a bright light on too many untold truths. Writers often write by hiding themselves between the pages of their books. There is no hiding in the shadows here, for we see the full evolution of Black's brilliance, his queerness, his blackness, his love of the written word. Engaging the familiar and unpacking the unfamiliar makes Daniel Black both witness and much needed prophet for our times. A book you will not want to put down and will be excited to share."

—Maryemma Graham, University of Kansas professor of English and founding director of Project on the History of Black Writing

BLACK ON BLACK
BLACK ON BLACK
BLACK ON BLACK
BLACK ON BLACK
BLACK ON BLACK

BLACK ON BLACK:

ON OUR RESILIENCE AND BRILLIANCE IN AMERICA

DANIEL BLACK

Recycling programs for this product may not exist in your area.

ISBN-13: 978-1-335-50822-5

Black on Black

First published in 2023. This edition published in 2025.

Hanover Square Press
22 Adelaide St. West, 41st Floor
Toronto, Ontario M5H 4E3, Canada
HanoverSqPress.com

Printed in U.S.A.

To every black activist, marcher, and protester whose name didn't go down in history.

Also by Daniel Black

Isaac's Song
Don't Cry for Me
They Tell Me of a Home
The Sacred Place
Perfect Peace
Twelve Gates to the City
The Coming
Listen to the Lambs

BLACK ON BLACK
BLACK ON BLACK
BLACK ON BLACK
BLACK ON BLACK
BLACK ON BLACK

TABLE OF CONTENTS

INTRODUCTION

What makes Daniel Black unique is his willingness to tell the difficult story. When, in 2010, he released his novel *Perfect Peace*, I knew we had an author whose literary skills matched the fierceness of his story. In this tale, Black introduces a child born male but raised as a girl. It was one of the first black trans novels in the country. That's who Black is—a disrupter of the status quo, a healer of the wounded, a mouthpiece of justice for the marginalized. In his work, readers get both the impact of first-rate literature and examples of humanity at its best and worst.

The essays in *Black on Black* are delicately and forcefully spun on the loom of Daniel Black's lived experiences. We are often, to borrow from one of Black's jegnas, Sister Sonia Sanchez, wounded in the houses of friends. Those wounds are in these pages, to be sure; but so, too, are the healing balms from the Gileads of black institutions, from the church to the school to the family and the countless other spaces beyond. Daniel Black is a reader's writer, requiring us to identify the inner sister, brother, mother, father, son, or daughter we too often fight fiercely to protect from a hostile world. For black people, this fight of self-protection is waged in a system of exploitation, dependent from its inception on ensuring, in matters large and small, that black lives do not matter.

Every word in *Black on Black* is fashioned from joy, pain, and tears. In these essays, Black urges readers to step beyond antiquated notions of masculinity. In essence, he wants spirit beings on the earth, people who don't diminish others as they exalt themselves. He wants divine souls who aren't afraid to disagree with power structures. He wants an America in which black people make the same assumptions about their citizenship as any other people. He wants the possibility that the American public school system and the American penal system believe that black life is worth living and saving. Put simply, he wants us free. And he's willing to pay for it.

Like August Wilson, Daniel Black takes his readers from country towns to ships bursting with enslaved and undefeated Africans, from the precarity of the materially unhoused and the biologically unsettled to terrors and triumphs found in forests bursting with lynching trees and hush harbors and concrete jungles leaving scars that obscure the bloody but unbowed presence of an unapologetically black humanity underneath. These essays trouble already troubled water. Black explains what happens to black institutions when they belie criticism. He also shows what happens when we don't have them. Most poignantly, he begs us to see people for who they are—not who we want or even need them to be.

At the same time, Black's personal wounds bleed all over the page. He asks readers to trace their source, to discover our fundamental flaws, our repeated mistakes, our beliefs that have cost us our dignity. And he dares us to heal, to insist on healing, although America holds for us no such requirement. Perhaps reading *Black on Black* is the healing.

After years of exploring our experiences through fiction, Daniel Black has at last chosen to narrate the black subject without the oblique safety of the novel. In doing so, Black returns blackness to spaces of promise, albeit ones fraught with continuing challenges of self-hatred, external assault, and temporary failures of will and vision. Longtime readers of Daniel Black will find something new in these explosive pages, a prophet who strips himself and his people bare in order to establish them as unashamed keepers of their own destiny.

The critical rememories in *Black on Black* connect to the beating heart of the black community, namely remade African cultural practices that keep our communities alive. If Du Bois's "two souls" has been mined alongside "the color line" as a signature metaphor from his 1903 epistle *The Souls of Black Folk*, it is the Africans' "one dark body" that is the signature metaphor of Black's epistle. Daniel Black believes in the dogged strength of that corporate concept of blackness, one he has uncovered and discovered through an unyielding life of study and practice. Following his introductory manifesto, the beating African heart of the blackness that informs *Black on Black* might be imagined as circulating the blood of his essays through four thematic chambers: The Black Self, The Black Church, The Black School, and Black Survival. The essays pump this blood of critical black rememory through the extensive network of vessels and capillaries that keep the one dark black collective body alive, self-governing and able to fend off the disease of white supremacy by navigating parasitic and unfailingly hostile social structures.

The Black Self is explored across physical, spiritual, cultural, and sociological dimensions in essays such as the unflinchingly vulnerable "Black, But Not Beautiful: An Aesthetic Dilemma"; "Massa, Don't Leave Me!", a candid confrontation of black self-contempt; "Dying to Be Loved," a startlingly honest exploration of and road map to communal redemption from the toxic intersection of condemned valences of sexuality and black male fatal self-harming; "The Power of *POSE*," an examination of black sexual denial in the 1980s and '90s and black performative responses that gave birth, once more, to new directions in popular culture; and "Nowhere to Hide (or The Dream of the Closet)," a self-revelation reminiscent of James Baldwin that will leave the reader transformed in its wake.

The Black Church is met both within and beyond its terms and limits by Black most directly in his essay "Prayer Won't Fix This: What to Do with the Black Church." His expansion of concepts of divine and holy word and practice ties classical and medieval Africa to the long black American liberation movement, and calls us to reimagine the institution.

Black Survival echoes most directly in essays on the forestalled racial reckoning engendered by the loss of black institutions in the wake of desegregation, including "Integration: A Failed Experiment" and "When WE See Us," Black's historical contextualization of Ava DuVernay's Central Park/Exonerated Five series. Additionally, "The Trial and Massacre of the Black Body" is a rehearsal of the litany of abuses that ties more familiar recent names of victims of state violence such as Bland, Floyd, and Taylor to a genealogy that includes Dred Scott, Homer Plessy, and others, before channeling another Southern ancestor, the Mississippian Ida Bell Wells, who, writing from Memphis, warned America of what will happen when black folk have run out of places to channel our rage. Not everyone will agree with Black's generous and African-centered reading of Kasi Lemmons's 2019 Harriet Tubman biopic in his essay "Harriet's Chariot," but the reader will be inspired to acquire a familiarity with Africana cultural ways of knowing, beyond the framing of blackness as racial, to be able to respond and debate.

The Black College is finally placed and discussed by an insider in its proper context in "The Beauty and Struggles of HBCUs." It is a well-known fact among those of us who teach in these schools that even black academics who attended them and who subsequently write about them from the imagined and desired safety and prestige of HWCUs exhibit no idea of what these schools are, face, and/or mean from the perspective of the teaching faculty who are the reason they exist and persist. Black uses his personal story to balance the spiritual, cultural, and intellectual value of the HBCU professoriat against the material cost of spending one's professional life engaged in the practice of truly teaching at an HBCU. Black's essay is a necessary corrective in an environment where "superstar faculty" are essentially being offered branding arrangements by a generation of neoliberal HBCU administrators and boards with no demonstrated connection or commitment to what Jelani Favors calls "the second curriculum" at these schools. Contingent and noncontingent faculty alike continue to shoulder the responsibility of teaching black students who, if they are lucky, have found their way to us from our counterparts in K-12 education who fostered their development while navigating equally detached bureaucracies. The reader will find a great deal in this essay to offer the "expensive hope" that sustains all of us who practice the teaching craft.

Open these pages. Read them. Tarry with them. Know them. Allow Daniel Omotosho Black to cover you in the blood of blackness. Everyone will find themselves in these essays if and when we bring our full and authentic selves to each page. With *Black on Black*, the mask is off. We thank the ancestors for this, the latest of Baba Omotosho's gifts.

Greg Carr
Howard University

REASONS I WRITE

I write because I believed I was ugly; then I wrote myself into beauty. I write because I hated who I was; then God told me I was divine and shame had no place in a divine soul. In exchange, I promised God to tell the truth—the real, naked, glorious truth—that we are all gods, made in the image of a perfect, marvelous Creator. I promised to tell that God is not concerned with flesh and blood, but with spiritual ecstasy shared between the living and the ought-to-be living. So, with pen and paper, I set about the duty of setting the world free.

I write because we rape. I write because we hurt. I write because some pain can't be described. It can only be felt in the marrow of a story or the lyrics of a song. I write for the boy who wanted to be a man but couldn't figure out how. Or the girl who dreamed of beauty but inherited brilliance instead. I write that they might not give up the fight. That they might know the failure is in others' eyes—not their being—it is in others' judgmental hearts—not their sacred difference. I write that they might live. That their stories might be holy and sacred, read by others standing at the cliff, weeping, trembling.

I write to soothe wounds too deep to heal. Day and night I write because precious blood streams from those who can't find God within. In every character, every plot, every description, every image I seek only to create a world full of gods—gay gods, lesbian gods, ant gods, leopard gods, tree gods, ocean gods, grass gods, elephant gods, but holy gods all—who share powers and kingdoms too secure for laws and limitations. I write that troubled black youth might happen past a mirror then dance at what they see.

I write that elders might know their lives were not in vain. I write to tell gay brothers they're straight, too. To shed light on the power of love and everyone's right to have it. I write to announce that, without forgiveness, there is no liberty. Its absence is bondage of the spirit, incarceration of the soul. Forgiveness is the only seed of transformation. It ushers you through the wilderness of chaos and pain, bruises and careless apologies, without the weight of empty promises. It teaches you that no one can control your happiness unless you surrender it.

I write to give readers permission to take it back. To tell the world to *kiss your ass* if it thinks you're going to die to satisfy other people's outdated, antiquated beliefs. To shout to the world "No fuckin' way!" when it tries to convince you that you're not supposed to be free.

This is why I write. To strengthen the strong and fortify the weak. To sing praises to those who died for those who wouldn't. To pay homage to those who declared, "I am black and beautiful!" long before most others agreed. To say thank you to men who love and honor women. To bow before women who love and honor men. To applaud the few who love and raise children they did not birth.

We've not taken the risk to strip ourselves naked before the world and stand in full confidence of what it beholds. We're not yet sure of our divinity, not yet convinced of our holiness, not yet persuaded that we're worthy of Heaven. We've not yet decided that, in our best, we're always enough.

So I write. And I'm going to write until the wind outsings my pen. If there is no paper, I shall use the wall. If there is no wall, I shall use my hand. If I must relinquish my hand, I shall use the very earth upon which we stand and scratch into the dust the sentiments of liberty.

There are triumphant stories to tell, unthinkable testimonies to hear. Stories some don't want to read, but everyone needs to heed. Stories that celebrate transgender angels and bisexual prophets. Stories of people we threw away who could've saved us. Stories of broken hearts, broken promises, broken dreams, broken ribs, broken spirits. Stories of victory and achievement against the odds. This is why I write. I have to write. Because America lies. It says black men don't love black men, and black children are inherently inferior. It says black women are fussy, naggy, bitchy, needy, shallow, and mouthy. Don't you see the lies? It needs these lies in order to boast itself the best country on the planet. That, too, is a lie—although it *could* be true—if America ever admitted who built the place. But that, my friend, is too much truth, and we all know what America does with truth.

So, until they love it, I write. For the obese and the anorexic, the joyless and the sorrowful. For the man too anguished to adorn. The woman too forgotten to mend. The child untouched and unpraised. I write for their hearts. Their precious, tender hearts. Each word is an invitation to believe a new thing, a different thing, a more marvelous, transformative thing that invites them to remove their mask and exist unashamed. I write because black people still speak of good hair and boast of minuscule strains of Indian blood in African veins. I write for those who birthed children then buried them too soon. Those who love so hard their hearts quiver. Those who *want* to love, but trauma disallows. Those who work miracles every day, but never get a crown. I write because we're still talking about Jesus, as if there's never been another, and, worse, we're still praising him for doing what most of us wouldn't do. Yes, I write because the kingdom of Heaven is at hand. Indeed, it has come and gone so many, many times, yet we keep looking *for* God while we're looking *at* God. So I write—that we might acquire eyes to see and ears to hear and voices with which to speak, and perhaps, then, finally, we'll discover that, together, we are the only God there is. But until that day, I write.

I write for imprisoned black souls, suffering for crimes they did not commit. Through words, I send them healing, reminders that the state can house their bodies but not their spirits. I write to reiterate that every great person was once bound—either by the state or themselves—Christ, King, Gandhi, Assata, Malcolm—for fear of what they knew, what they wouldn't do, what they might sacrifice for the world's freedom. I write because my grandfather couldn't. My father could but wouldn't. My brothers can but won't. There are more children coming. More ideas to birth, more words we haven't found. The word is life! It is blood in the imagination! Food to the starving soul. This is why I write!

I write to remind us that every day without love is a day wasted. It is a sunrise dishonored, a breathless, lifeless existence that only the unintelligent can endure. I write for the insecure, the inept, the uncertain, the self-doubting, the woefully timid; the thick, the husky, the thin, the tentative, the spiritually paraplegic, the emotionally palsied. Through books, I seek to banish hatred and pursue its antidote. This is why I write.

I write to hold the hand of the depressed and the dying, the lonely and the suicidal. I have to write. It is my calling, the price I pay for the breath I breathe.

I want blackness to bloom all over this land and mend what whiteness has broken. I want people to love the stranger, honor the ex-con, respect the sex worker. To assume their humanity regardless of their appearance or station. To know that every life is worth its breath. We all are. But sometimes we're not so sure. So, for those in-between times, I write. Until people stop justifying their existence to people who don't matter. Until Americans admit that some Americans came in chains. Until men fight for women's reproductive rights. Until we stop believing wealth equals human value. Until we "let everything that hath breath" speak for itself. Until we discover that as long as there are books, there is everlasting life! This is why I write.

We've crowned someone else our God. We've abandoned our ancestors in exchange for dollars but no sense. We've deserted dreams because others couldn't comprehend them. We've let daddy's failures and momma's shortcomings define who and what we are. But they, Momma and Daddy, were only hills and mountains to climb in order to learn how to climb, for Heaven is a high place. I write that we might *make* a Heaven instead of simply waiting for one. I also write to encourage Justice to fight on, to know that winning happens in many ways and sometimes without celebration. If Justice quits, we all lose. If Justice fails, we shall rally behind her and lift her high. This is why I write. Because we are custodians of this planet, stewards of mercy and kindness who owe each other a bright, uninhibited "Good Morning." Then we'll rise like the morning sun and comfort like an evening breeze and satisfy like a shading tree and be, finally, whatever God is.

This is why I write. All you have to do…is read.

WHEN I WAS A BOY

There will be no children to surround my deathbed, no grandchildren to reminisce on holidays with Pawpaw, no great-grandchildren to carry on my name. That's not why I came.

I came to reproduce ideas—not people. To show the world what God looks like in the flesh. To remind black people of their majesty. To discover why Africans had to be enslaved and dispersed throughout a world that *still* doesn't know who we are.

I spent years longing and begging and pleading and hoping to fall in love when, according to most, I was unlovable. God had not made me what I was. Somehow, I had sneaked into this universe, unsanctioned by the angels, and thus unapplauded. This is what the people said. They even agreed that, if I didn't change, Hell would be my home. Only the Devil would know me in eternity. I had no choice but to believe them. There was no other God to pray to, no other deity who might plead my case. I asked about other gods, and people said there was only one. All these people in the world and only one God? If only I'd been free enough to know better.

I lived in bondage. My people came enslaved. Everything about us was confined, including our imaginations. We were duped into leaving our own gods behind and bowing before entities that had no power at all. But, over time, our belief in those gods empowered them to capture our minds and rearrange our faith in ourselves. Now, when we close our eyes and pray, whiteness cloaks our ethereal space. There is hardly any blackness at all. They took our names, our rituals, our land, our tongues…small wonder we love their gods instead of our own.

Yet here I am. Black and clear that God looks like me. As a boy, I wasn't so sure. I wasn't like other boys. I loved pretty things and longed only for my mother's bosom. I didn't want to be a man. The men I knew weren't upstanding or virtuous. They didn't love God; they loved themselves. They beat women and demeaned each other. They whistled at teenage girls and gambled paychecks away. They sat in pulpits without the requisite integrity. I wasn't proud of them; I didn't want to be among them. They drank until their good senses faded away. They belittled sensitive boys, calling us names that made us cry. I dreaded their coming like an impending storm. Violence signified their being. Whipping, beating, lashing, mocking others filled their pastimes. I couldn't imagine them as God. But I wanted to. I'd be one of them one day.

But hopefully not like them. I wanted women to sing my praises, children to anticipate my approach with joy, men to envy my character. I wanted God to boast of my excellence, to tell the angels I was one of a kind. I didn't want to be feared to be followed. I didn't want control over people's bodies. I didn't want privilege without honor.

I wanted to love without limitation. I wanted girls to trust me because I respected them. I wanted to know the warmth of boys' hands. I wanted to braid girls' hair because I loved beauty. And I wanted a father who could see God *in* me and God *as* me. Yet I didn't get any of these things. After all, I was a boy.

In high school, I read books and pieced quilts and baked cakes and wrote in diaries. I scratched Grandma's scalp and danced around her living room like Alvin Ailey and Gene Anthony Ray. I learned to knit and crochet when other boys were coon hunting and chewing tobacco. I sang the lead in church choir and cried when Nettie and Celie reunited. I took French and home ec instead of shop and engineering. But I could've done engineering. Math came easily for me. It just didn't invite the sharing of my heart, so I abandoned it. I painted my nails once, just to see what they would look like, then, not knowing of fingernail polish remover, I soaked my hands in gasoline before my father got home. My brothers showed me *Hustler* and *Playboy* pictures that didn't elicit my erection. I was a failure. No wet dreams, no masturbation, no jokes about boobs and ass. I was a weirdo. A fuckin' freak. A nobody. A disappointment to a nation of men.

Yet I insisted on living. I joined a church and met a God whom I didn't admire. People said He didn't like me either. In fact, they said He wasn't a man at all, but clearly He had preferred pronouns. When I called Him *She*, preachers reprimanded me and said the Bible confirmed His maleness, His headship over humanity. Of course it did, I said, since men wrote the book and therefore named all the characters. Yet why couldn't God be a woman? What did we lose by considering it possible? My grandmother was far more godlike than my grandfather. People laughed at the innocence of my youth, but they didn't join my protest. After a while, they stared at me with disdain and rebuke. A few told me to shut up and seek God's face. I did that, but couldn't find it. Not back then. So I just shut up. But I didn't stop wondering.

I soon learned that people wanted unenlightened black boys. Unkind black boys. Weed-smoking black boys. Half-drunk, baby-producing black boys. Girl-chasing black boys. People applauded black boys with faded cuts and cascading locks—not mounds of nappy hair resting atop an uneven head. They embraced boys with mediocre grades and unexceptional character. Boys who solicited cheerleaders but never themselves cheered for anyone. Those were the boys who made mothers smile and fathers boast. Those were the boys girls gave themselves to. The boys other boys privately desired. These boys became preachers and pastors, civil rights leaders and college professors, news anchors and greasy mechanics. Black people in my day wanted black boys whose gifts they could commodify, boys whose talents might one day make them millions. At twenty-five, I was a poor writer. Nothing to be proud of. Not yet.

But something about language buttressed my self-worth. In words, I heard the timbre of the real God's voice, the frantic fluttering of angel's wings, and I knew that if I could gather words into my mouth, I could speak my own worth. I could mix subjects and objects and verbs and phrases and unspeak what the world had spoken about me. I knew that if I could master the word, I could reconstruct the heart I had grown to hate. So I read books and pamphlets and *Reader's Digest* and flyers and obituaries and church anniversary programs and automobile manuals and the parts of the Bible I liked and newspapers and coupons and grocery store receipts and junk mail and birth certificates and birthday party announcements.

I read recipes and cereal boxes and encyclopedias and church hymnals and Sunday school primers and shopping advertisements and, of course, library books.

With all that reading came questions no one could answer. Like why would God put people in paradise then tempt them to ruin it? Or why couldn't humans eat from the tree of good and evil *and* be all-knowing? What was wrong with all-knowingness? Was God insecure? Or why did women take men's last names although most men wouldn't take theirs? Or what personal pleasure did white crewmen get from throwing black bodies into the Atlantic Ocean? Isn't that rather sadistic and evidence of a soulless people? Or why didn't men wear dresses, especially in the summer? Lord knows it was hot enough. Or why didn't men accompany each other to the bathroom like women? And why do men stand up to pee? Isn't sitting far more comfortable? Every time I asked these questions, people said I was *too smart for my own good*—whatever that meant. Some accused me of thinking I was *better than other folks*. Actually, I thought I was far worse.

Since many desirable black men sang, I tried that route as a way toward acceptance and celebration. Yet something went wrong. I think my range was too high. No bass resonance, no sign that the seed of a man was in me. I sang a natural-voice soprano so loud and strong that most turned away when I performed. My flailing arms didn't help. Nor did my trembling vibrato, which I thought people loved. And they did—but not in a boy. They wanted Barry White or Marvin Gaye or Luther Vandross. Those were not my idols. When I practiced in the barn, I sang along with Patti LaBelle and Vanessa Bell Armstrong, Chaka Khan and Natalie Cole. If I could hit their notes—and often I did—I felt triumphant.

Still, no praise. I couldn't figure it out. What did people want? I had straight As, no criminal record, no illegitimate children, no lifetime scars. Then I admitted what I already knew: they wanted a man.

So I gave them one.

I started smoking weed and hanging out in bars and alleys where masculinity was free for the taking. I started flirting with girls and having sex to prove my prowess. I started pimp walking like Denzel and holding my head like Idris Elba. I cut my hair down to a smooth fade and straightened the top naps with a nylon wave cap. I threw away those formfitting jeans, the ones I liked so well, and began sagging along with all the other homeboys. My grandmother said I looked like a fool. My father said it was about time. I didn't like what I was becoming, but I *was* becoming, and that was the goal.

In exchange for masculinity, I stopped reading books. I stopped analyzing movies. I stopped dancing before full-length mirrors. I stopped playing for the choir. Stopped scratching Grandma's scalp. Stopped crying at others' abuse. Stopped caring about women's issues. Stopped cooking, especially baking. Stopped going to church. I guess I stopped acting like a faggot. Boys were relieved. Daddy told his friends, "I know what I raised!" Momma thanked God that prayer changes things.

Yet when I got to college, I dropped the charade. It just didn't make sense anymore. Life-changing books found me and restored my senses. Hermann Hesse's *Siddhartha* and Zora Neale Hurston's *Their Eyes Were Watching God*. Chinua Achebe's *Things Fall Apart* and Ann Petry's *The Street*. We read essays by Joan Didion, Langston Hughes, Alain Locke, and Audre Lorde. Poems by Paul Laurence Dunbar, Sonia Sanchez, John

Milton, and Shakespeare. I discovered the depth of my self-imposed incarceration. My chains fell off, as Baldwin might say. Each text summoned the unashamed expression of my soul. I wept to be reunited with myself.

One short story in particular set me free. It's Arna Bontemps's "A Summer Tragedy." The story explores black agency in a time when black people weren't supposed to have it. The narrative centers around an old, poor, disenfranchised black couple who decide how and when to die. They don't wait for Death to come and snatch their lives away. Instead, they dress in their Sunday best and intentionally drive off a steep cliff, meeting Death on their own terms. I understood that. I had met Death before—when I thought I was tired of living. But Death wouldn't take me. "You haven't fulfilled your contract yet," he said. So I stayed and grew into an adult.

But was I a man?

One night on Clark College's quad, I met a brother who made me answer that question. It was after midnight. He sauntered easily, going nowhere really, and found me drowning for attention. I spoke first. Or maybe he did. I don't remember. But our conversation changed me forever.

We shot the breeze for a minute or two, then he sat next to me on a bench beneath a lamppost and asked, "Who are you?"

I told him my name, where I'm from, basic things like that.

He said, "Naw, man. I'm askin' who are you?"

I didn't understand. He shook his head.

"Your name is what we call you. Your home is where you're from. I want to know who you are, why you exist."

I didn't know. Everywhere I searched within, I found only vacant spaces.

He chuckled and said, "I'll see you around, man. Next time, have an answer."

I sat there, by myself, until the sun rose the next morning. I'd never known such turmoil, such spiritual anxiety. All night long I turned his question over in my mind until realizing that this was what I'd come to college for. It was my job to decide who I was—not someone else's privilege to tell me. That was the error I'd made my whole life—waiting for others to confirm my right to exist. I understood now.

Several nights later, that brother and I met again on the same bench. It felt like time had returned us to the earlier moment, and once again, it was only him and me.

He approached with a smile and a warm demeanor. Then, without hesitation or self-consciousness, he touched my hand briefly, and my spirit vibrated within.

"Well?" he said.

I nodded and offered, "I'm a spirit, come to show people how to love."

He chuckled. "Yes, my brother. Now you got it." Then he left.

I never saw him again.

THE TRIAL AND MASSACRE OF THE BLACK BODY

On April 20, 2021, I sat before the TV screen, chewing my bottom lip until it bled. I, and so many others around the nation, waited to hear the fate of Derek Chauvin, the smug-ass white dude who had killed George Floyd. Darnella Frazier, an innocent bystander, had caught the murder on tape, so this was supposedly an open-and-shut case. Or was it? Truth is, I wasn't so sure. America has always been the master of social illusion—casting truth as lies and lies as truth, convincing citizens that they didn't see what they saw. It's a cultural switcheroo that slaveholders began and modern politicians continue. It's in the very fabric of America. That's why this nation calls itself the Land of Liberty while perpetuating most people's bondage.

It's no secret that countless black lives have been lost in the last decade as white police declare their innocence. This isn't new either. What's new is their ability to do so even as video evidence says otherwise. The question becomes not whether a black person is dead, but whether the police we *see* committing the act will be held responsible. And, to be honest, the real question is whether a white man can *ever* be guilty of killing a black man. That's what I was waiting to see. It's an absurd question because racism is absurd.

I kept reviewing the facts: white Minneapolis police officers, led by Derek Chauvin, wrestled George Floyd to the ground, supposedly for trying to spend fake money in a nearby corner store, then, deeming him "unruly"—this is how the bullshit always begins—they felt the need to "subdue" him until help arrived. This isn't what the video shows. With Floyd on the ground, unable to resist arrest, Chauvin casually and arrogantly leans his knee into Floyd's neck, pressing down for more than nine minutes as Floyd whispers, "I can't breathe." That's what infuriated so many people. Chauvin saw Floyd's life seep away as he restricted his breath, and he didn't care. A black man's death didn't trouble him one bit. Not one bit.

The difference this time was that blacks and many liberal whites were equally enraged. Some of those whites made their way onto the jury. Yet would this be enough? Was history about to change? Could an imperfect black man's life shatter the shield of cultural protection that surrounds white male patriarchy and power? I wasn't convinced. In fact, I was prepared for Chauvin to be exonerated. Yet when the jury convicted him, I gasped. Then I sighed and shook my head. I wasn't happy. This verdict was too exceptional for me to be happy. But I was encouraged that perhaps, just perhaps, America was beginning to change.

Black bodies have been hunted and murdered since the days of slavery, and once police departments were formed in the 1830s and '40s, they assumed the same role—to protect precious white citizens from the threat of black criminality. Still, because the murder of George Floyd was so blatant *and* caught on tape, we hoped his killer would be convicted. And he was. Yet our joy was ephemeral.

We knew this conviction wouldn't change America fundamentally. It wouldn't alter the system of black suspicion and murder that has characterized this country from its beginning. It would *not* mean that police would stop killing us. The Chauvin decision simply allowed us to exhale for a second.

And only a second. For even during the trial, on April 11, a police officer named Kim Potter, in Minneapolis no less, shot and killed Daunte Wright—a twenty-year-old black man—by mistakenly shooting him instead of tasing him. These stories are all too familiar to black people, who wonder why shooting is always law enforcement's first response. Then, on April 20, the same day the jury convicts Chauvin for murder, police in Columbus, Ohio, shoot and kill Ma'Khia Bryant, a sixteen-year-old black girl who had called the police herself in search of protection from a group of bullying girls. Police cam shows Ma'Khia with a knife in her hand, lunging toward another girl, when an officer shoots her. Responses from public officials and media personalities have been mixed. Some justify the shooting by suggesting that, in such volatile moments, police make split-second decisions that any other human being might make. Others wonder, once again, why shooting to kill is always the first response when a black body is involved.

And if this isn't enough police controversy, on December 5, 2020, a black man, Caron Nazario, in full military regalia, was pulled over, pepper-sprayed, and knocked to the ground simply because he was driving a new SUV with a temporary paper tag. He had also decided to drive to a well-lit gas station about a mile away before he pulled over. This was especially horrifying because it demonstrated, for the whole world to see, that blackness trumps the honor of military status in America. I thought of all the black soldiers who have fought in America's wars—from the American Revolution to the

Afghanistan conflict—yet returned home to racial abuse and unfettered discrimination. I mean, can you imagine how insulted and demoralized black soldiers have felt after putting their lives on the line to protect *every* American, only to be targeted as black and therefore abusable? It's indisputable evidence that race is the guiding trope in America, and that as long as one is black, one is unprotected—even if one bears the regalia and insignia of American military democracy.

Truth is, nothing saves a black body from violent public (and private) scrutiny. Since our arrival, we, the black people of this land, have been searched and questioned in ways that leave us on trial continuously. The auction block itself was a kind of trial—a place where the worth and value of black bodies was publicly displayed and decided upon. I might even argue that the current number of black street murders today is the inevitable outcome of a country that could at one point institutionalize and culturally validate the auction block. Put simply, the fact that black bodies were once bought and sold in the American marketplace, whether for labor or sexual gratification, means that they could also be destroyed—if they didn't perform their imagined duty—without owners' fear of legal or moral reprisal. It also means that recognizing these bodies as "human" would prove difficult for future generations of white Americans because their introduction to blackness was by its utility—not its humanity. In other words, seeing black people as equal beings has been an uphill battle, even for liberal whites I contend, precisely because the public image of blackness has often been shaped by its serviceability to whiteness instead of the glory of its own human merit. We must remember that, by definition, America is a white supremacist idea. We know this because, in 1776, white colonial settlers conceived their own liberation while holding black bodies enslaved and subject to their economic dreams. This simply means that black bodies continued to be publicly commodified as America's founding fathers—many of whom owned those bodies—constructed a new world and way of life without black inclusion.

Even today, everywhere we go and in everything we do, black people are constantly surveilled, made to question our very existence. It's 2022 and the general public is still surprised and celebratory when a black person achieves what white folks have been achieving for decades. This is evidenced by the fact that, as a country, we believe the majority of black people to be underprivileged instead of recognizing, finally, that most whites are *overprivileged.*

As early as 1781, court cases involving black bodies have been adjudicated in American courtrooms. The said Mumbet, a black woman enslaved in the household of Colonel John Ashley in upper Massachusetts, sued him for her freedom. She fled from the estate because of a run-in with Mrs. Ashley—Mumbet shielded and protected a young girl from the mistress, who meant to strike the child with a heated shovel—but John wanted her back. She overheard a reading of the Massachusetts state constitution and decided that the liberty it promised should be hers as well. So she summoned the legal representation of Theodore Sedgwick, an abolitionist lawyer, who argued convincingly that all people of the state were free under the new state constitution. They won their case, and Mumbet went free. She renamed herself Elizabeth Freeman, to signify, like so many enslaved people after her, that she would never be enslaved again.

Yet I wonder what other Africans in the area were thinking or hoping as the case unfolded. Just as we sat glued to the televised trial of Derek Chauvin, I'm sure Africans in Great Barrington, Massachusetts, worked and prayed nervously in 1781, waiting to hear about the day's events in the trial of Mumbet. Was she a fool for taking a white man to court? Was she a fool for trusting a white lawyer to represent her? History claims that she could neither read nor write, which may very well have been true. But this does not mean she was unintelligent. In other words, the problem with this historical legal moment is that credit is given to Sedgwick for arguing the case when, in fact, Mumbet conceptualized the challenge. She approached *him* and sought representation. She must've known or at least imagined the potential cost of her behavior. She had to be aware that the legal system was not designed to protect her. Yet she must also have hoped that righteousness would prevail, if she summoned the same dream of liberty as her owner's. So that's what she did. However, because she was black and therefore assumed inferior, the praise goes to the white man who defended her. When they won, I imagine local blacks skeptically happy—the way we were when we heard the Chauvin verdict—because they surely knew that ultimately the judicial system aimed not to free them but to uphold its own principles and values, and if blacks benefited, very well. But if they didn't, it was all the same.

Throughout American history, black people's freedom—or their right to have it—has been addressed in countless court cases, most often to their immeasurable disappointment. Ultimately, the real question—Are black people truly human?—lurked beneath legal discourse and colored the judge's and jury's ultimate decision. Take, for instance, the 1839 trial of enslaved Africans aboard the *Amistad*. This ship was seized in

American waters, and captured Africans were detained in jail until the American government could "decide" if they should be free or not. On January 13, 1840, Judge Andrew Judson declared that these enslaved Mende people should be returned to their homeland, for they had been taken illegally. This decision was disapproved of by US President Martin Van Buren, who had hoped to extradite the Africans back to Cuba. The case went to the Supreme Court on March 9, 1841, argued by John Quincy Adams, and once again bound Africans were granted their freedom and thus returned to Africa on, ironically, the *Gentleman*. My issue is that white supremacy had the power to determine whether or not they *should* be free, whether or not they *would* be seen and treated as human. In other words, the problem is not the outcome of the trial; it's the need for the trial itself. It's the fact that black people's existence is always a question in America, always something to contemplate and ponder, as if blackness needs the gift of white sanction for its legitimacy. How do you steal a people from their homeland then wonder if they should be returned? And who are you to decide? These fundamental questions rest at the foundation of white supremacist thinking and cause black bodies to be forever examined for the *possibility* of humanness. Far too often, black bodies have appeared in court not because of a crime they've committed, but because they dared assume themselves American citizens. George Floyd did not die because he broke the law; he died because he seemingly wouldn't obey and submit to white male authority. That's why he died. That's always why we die.

Dred Scott, in the 1840s, was disobedient too. In essence, he sued his so-called owner, Irene Emerson, in 1846, claiming that because he had been in free territory—Illinois—he was a free man. This would've been a no-brainer if Scott had been white. But he wasn't. He was a Negro whose humanity most white Americans had not agreed to. The initial court found in his favor, but the decision was overturned by the higher Missouri Supreme Court in 1852. The trial went to the US Supreme Court in February of 1856 where, once again, Scott lost his freedom. Yet, most egregiously, Irene remarried, and she and her husband sold Scott to abolitionists who then granted him his freedom. In other words, they set Scott free when *they* felt ready to. They had to prove to him that he did not, and would not ever, have power to litigate against whiteness. Once he got clear of that, he could go.

Ironically, Scott had tried to purchase his and his family's freedom long before he sued for it. Yet what does it mean for a man to purchase *himself*? How does he buy himself from another man? He doesn't. Not if he's recognized as human. And therein is the American dilemma for people of African descent: our personhood is always discursive, always uncertain, always a public dilemma. It means we are always for sale, always a negotiation away from some type of bondage, always a conversation concerning intellectual possibility and capability. See, if America ever concedes black humanity, it must also concede white culpability of centuries of evil. And since that's not going to happen, black bodies keep bearing the weight of the question of who gets to be human and thus divine in this modern age.

Plessy v. Ferguson is yet another legal moment in which black humanity found itself on trial. This case involved Homer Plessy—a near-white black man—who, in 1892, refused to sit in a railcar specifically designated for Negroes. Plessy sued, arguing that his constitutional rights had been violated. The

Supreme Court ruled that a legal distinction based upon color was not unconstitutional. Said differently, it was perfectly acceptable to provide separate public accommodations based upon racial difference—as long as those accommodations were equal. Of course they never were. The Supreme Court surely never thought they would be. The point of this trial was to validate segregation, to confirm to the general white public that they didn't have to respect black people in their everyday lives. It was really about elevating whiteness to an untouchable status while assuring that black flesh would always get the lash if it ever assumed itself equal. Evidence of this lies in the fact that Homer Plessy was seven-eighths Caucasian and only one-eighth black. In appearance, he looked like a white man. But that didn't matter. He claimed blackness and that was enough in the American judicial imagination to chastise him. Said differently, the court system was legislating the place of blackness in society—not its relationship to one pseudo-black man. The Supreme Court laid the foundation for black bodies to continue to be dissected, long into the twentieth century, even after the Fourteenth Amendment, ratified in 1868, guaranteed equal protection under the law.

The idea of "separate but equal," which the Plessy case introduces, is the single most rhetorically racist discourse ever articulated in America. If things are truly equal, their proximity becomes irrelevant. This phrase functioned between Reconstruction and the 1960s civil rights movement as an imaginative pacifier to keep black people hoping for something that would never come—equality. Part of the shame is that black people actually believed in it and worked hard to practice it. Most whites didn't live in fear of dangerous black people or pray that black people wouldn't destroy their communities.

When whites entered segregated black neighborhoods, they weren't raped or beaten or called demeaning names. But when blacks entered white spaces, we experienced all of the above. Consider the nine black students who, in 1957, integrated Central High School in Little Rock, Arkansas. In fact, consider any black students who integrated any white school anywhere in the United States in the 1950s and '60s! They were hosed down, trampled, humiliated, and cursed at. This was always the case when uninvited black bodies infiltrated white spaces. Yet when whites penetrated black neighborhoods, they weren't treated this way. Black mobs didn't beat them simply for being white. Or for conducting business with a black patron. Or for sitting in a black restaurant. Or for drinking water from a "black only" fountain. (Wait! Was there ever such a thing?) Blacks didn't debase whites because they had treated blacks poorly, although such could've easily been justified. It's when blacks entered white segregated spaces that the facade of "separate but equal" was exposed. Thousands of black people lost their lives simply walking through white neighborhoods. This proves that the "separate but equal" edict was a deception from the beginning. You can't treat someone "equally" if you don't honor them. Yet honoring black life has never been a cultural or legal mandate for white America. The US Supreme Court's construction of the separate but equal rhetoric was the lip service offered to black people as a way to suggest that their citizenship was on the way—if they'd just be patient. It was the discursive prank the legal system connived to assure that whites had no obligation to treat black bodies with any respect whatsoever. What it proved was that American court systems had learned the art of verbal subterfuge in relation to black public resistance. They had learned to speak what they thought blacks wanted to hear, without implicating themselves as the perpetuators of violence and racist ideology.

Consider also the 1955 murder of Emmett Till. This black boy, a mere fourteen years old, lost his life because he wouldn't submit to Southern rules of racial engagement. He spoke to a white woman, Carolyn Bryant, as if he were a human being, created equally, and for that he had to pay. Her husband, Roy, and his half brother J. W. Milam abducted Till and beat him to death then gouged out his left eye. By doing so, they sent a message to the black community: "If you won't honor the boundaries of white supremacy, we are prepared to destroy you. Completely." Yes, there was a trial. And this time, because of the advent of the television, the world was watching. An all-white, all-male jury found both men not guilty. The black community shuddered with rage. The world was shocked. How could no one be guilty when a black child's body had been mangled and mutilated? Emmett's mother, Mamie Till, said the trial had been a farce. Roy and J.W. showed no remorse whatsoever. In fact, some months later, they sold their story to *Look* magazine for $4,000.

It's what they did to Till's body that troubles me. They beat him so badly his mother hardly recognized him. And they beat him that way in order to prove that the cost of black disobedience will be the dismantling of the black body. No white man is guilty when he puts a black person back in his place. This, in fact, is his duty, his social contract with supremacy, the way he undergirds the prowess of the American empire. Because of double jeopardy, Roy and J.W. couldn't be tried again after their confession, but it wouldn't have mattered anyway. They had corrected a black boy's "error"—his assumption of his own humanness—and Mississippi, indeed the white South, was proud they'd done it. Yet Mamie Till turned their trick on its head. These white men had used her son's body to reinscribe the limits of black agency in the South, so she used it at an open-casket funeral to show the world the diabolical nature of white supremacy. Media sources worldwide ran the picture of Till's contorted face and thus exposed what black Americans always knew—that their bodies bear the cost of their defiance. And, worse, whites seem to enjoy making them pay.

This was the horror of George Floyd's death—that Officer Chauvin killed him slowly, easily, enjoyably. He smiled, it seemed, as Floyd's breath expired. Chauvin demonstrated no fear that, in killing a black man, he'd be in trouble. His self-righteous expression makes clear that, as a white man, he felt exonerated before the crime was even committed. He entertained no notion, surely, that he would *ever* be on trial for the murder of a nigga. That's why he looked into the cell phone camera casually; there was nothing to fear. Yes, the world was watching, as it had been watching in 1955, but so what? Everyone knows the cost of a black man's defiance; Chauvin was simply making Floyd pay. And he did. Just like Emmett Till's killers. And usually the courts support this heinous behavior. Indeed, Till's jury deliberated only sixty-seven minutes. It took that long, one juror admitted, because "we stopped to drink pop." The life of a Negro boy meant absolutely nothing to them. They used his body as text upon which to inscribe their fury that a black person actually believed he had the right to talk *any kind of way* to a white woman. Till's brutalized form functioned as the metaphor of correction for black people who might've thought they were above the rules of white supremacy. And, again, most courts over the years have backed this correction.

Fast-forward to the spring of 1991, and, once again, a black body is on trial. Perhaps Rodney King didn't know the Emmett Till case. Perhaps he thought time had granted him agency Till didn't possess. Perhaps he believed that, finally, the public lynching of black people was over. Whatever he believed, he was wrong, and LA police proved it. We know the story: Rodney King was a black man on parole who led white policemen on a high-speed chase. They finally caught him and beat him to a pulp. They fractured his skull, broke a few bones, and left him with permanent brain damage. These officers were charged and taken to trial. In April of 1992, they were acquitted by a jury with no black representation. (One juror was biracial.) The question is, why did they beat Rodney King that way? The answer: because he dared believe he could outwit them. It's the same reason slave catchers beat slaves if they were caught trying to escape. Their ego was bruised. How dare a nigga believe he could outrun, outsmart, outfox a white pursuer! Catching him or her wasn't enough. They had to be taught not to *try*.

What jarred black sensibility about Rodney King's beating is that we saw it—live on tape. The whole world saw it, and that's what made outraged black people believe something would be different. This might've been the first time police were caught on tape beating a black subject. Their guilt was obvious; their crime indisputable. Yet, somehow, they were exonerated. We, the black community, were told that what we saw we didn't see. Our eyes were not trustworthy. Truth could not be extracted via observation. We were made to feel dumb, unintelligent, and unable to trust the reliability of our own faculties. We knew now that the criminal justice system was playing games with our lives, and we didn't intend to take that shit. So we rioted. We tore up South Central Los Angeles as a means of saying "Stop fucking with us! We're not stupid!" We had no other recourse. If the law won't protect us, what else could we do?

Black people enjoyed a short legal respite when, in 1995, O.J. was found not guilty of murdering his ex-wife and her friend, both of whom were white. Every black person I knew watched as police chased that white SUV on television. Then, on the day of the verdict, black people huddled around television sets once again to see if a black man might win in America. We did not necessarily believe O.J. to be *innocent*; really, the hope was that a black body wouldn't have to die just because a white body had been killed. In other words, black people rooted for O.J. simply because we wanted to be found "not guilty" for a change—whether it was true or not. Why is this important? Because, for centuries, we'd been found "guilty" when it wasn't true at all. We wanted proof that at least it was *possible* for a black body not to die in confrontation with a white one. So black people rejoiced at the verdict for what it implied—that a black body *could* be set free if charged of a crime against whiteness. That alone was success. We made no arguments about O.J.'s character.

Then, in 2013, George Zimmerman was acquitted for the murder of seventeen-year-old Trayvon Martin, and we were back where we started. Once again, black folks sat, fingers crossed, before television sets, hoping that, finally, a dead black boy would be vindicated. He wasn't. Zimmerman got off because of the "stand your ground" statute in Florida, which allows a person to use deadly force against another person if they feel threatened. It seemed impossible that a 190-pound, grown-ass man felt threatened by a 150-pound black boy, but that's what they argued. Trayvon wore a set of headphones and ate a bag of Skittles, suggesting he was minding his own business, but I guess that didn't matter. Zimmerman shot him anyway. The subtext here is that black life, even a black child's life, is always tenuous in America, always subject to the whims of someone else's perception. Zimmerman did what Roy Bryant did—he destroyed the seed of black manhood before it could bloom. And the law thanked him for it.

Then, on August 9, 2014, in the city of Ferguson, Missouri, Officer Darren Wilson murdered eighteen-year-old Michael Brown Jr. Witnesses said Brown was shot with his hands in the air. Officer Wilson contradicted this testimony, and a grand jury believed him. Thus, they cleared him of all charges.

My frustration is how public officials treated Brown's body. They left him in the street, like roadkill, for four hours before they removed him. What possible excuse could justify such reproachable behavior? It's the notion that Michael Brown was a nigga—a thing, an object to be destroyed, a threat to be dissolved—that allowed the St. Louis County Police Department to leave his body baking in the sun as if he didn't matter. Any excuse given by any authority cannot explain why this young man's body lay in the middle of the street for four hours. Sure, it was the weekend. Sure, there was tension between the medical examiner's office and the police department. Sure, there were other public disturbances to attend to that day. But here's the question: Would a white boy's body have been left similarly under the same circumstances? I don't think so. Neighbors didn't either. That's why they almost rioted, although to no avail. Brown lay lifeless, probably like

Emmett Till did, until the message to black America was clear: *Do not ever challenge white authority. You are guaranteed to lose.*

Lest one think this happens only to black men, ask Sandra Bland what happened to her. She was pulled over for, supposedly, a routine traffic violation on July 10, 2015, and somehow the encounter escalated into a physical confrontation. According to Texas state trooper Brian Encinia, Bland was verbally resistant. Then, when asked to exit the car, she kicked him. Cam recorder footage showed Bland on the ground, pleading for her life, telling Encinia that she is epileptic. He said, sarcastically, "Good." She was arrested, of course, and taken to the Waller County Jail, where she was put in a cell by herself because they feared she might hurt others. In other words, they isolated her. This was the first move to decimate her body. They left her alone with no witnesses. I cannot say definitively what they did to her, but I *can* say the stage was set for them to do whatever they chose. And somehow, three days later, her body was found hanging from the ceiling. Her death was classified as a suicide. The black community shook its head. No one could prove anything counter to what officials reported, but this scene was suspect to say the least: a "mouthy" black woman argues with police and "ends up" dead. Even if she was belligerent and didn't submit easily, why did she have to die? Black people keep forgetting, it seems, that resistance to white authority equals black death. This is how "safety" is maintained in America.

That's why, on March 13, 2020, police shot and killed Breonna Taylor. They were searching for a criminal—her boyfriend, Kenneth Walker. He, believing the officers were intruders, gave a warning shot and hit one of the officers in the leg. They returned thirty-two shots, six of which killed

Taylor instead. The absurdity of this is profound. Whether these officers announced themselves or not does not answer the question of why Breonna Taylor is dead. The answer is in the illusion of safety police are paid to maintain. And, in America, safety often means protection from the threat of blackness. None of the officers were charged in Breonna's death, although one was charged with "wanton endangerment" of Taylor's neighbors—her *white* neighbors. How much more unfair could a justice system be? A black woman is dead and there are no charges, while whites next door feel merely endangered and someone must pay?

This reminds me of the way many black women have been tried (and punished) for their association with certain "criminalized" black men. Take Nat Turner's wife, Cherry, for instance. Sources say she was beaten and tortured for information concerning her fugitive husband's whereabouts after his deadly 1831 rebellion. From what we know, she did not relent, but certainly she paid the price for having loved a "dangerous" black man. Or consider the tragic story of Harry and Harriette Moore in Florida in the early 1950s. Harry founded the Brevard County NAACP chapter, a fact that sparked fury in the local KKK chapter. As a result, they planted a bomb beneath the master bedroom of the Moore household and killed Harry and wounded Harriette enough that she died nine days later. She was simply a casualty in the KKK's desire to ruin her husband and his realm of influence. American penal authorities are more than willing to destroy a black woman if she hinders their capture of a threatening black man. Her death will be understood as a tertiary necessity in keeping America "safe."

Someone had better be glad the jury found Derek Chauvin guilty of all charges. Black people are sick and tired of surrendering our bodies to the maintenance of white supremacy. And even since the verdict, black bodies have *still* died at the hands of police. One day soon, other bodies are going to die, too. And they won't be black this time.

PRAYER WON'T FIX THIS: WHAT TO DO WITH THE BLACK CHURCH

I was raised in the black church. So were all the other children in my community. From as early as I can remember, it shaped our lives and our mythology of the afterlife. Everything we did centered around the church: Sunday school, Wednesday Bible study, Saturday morning youth choir rehearsal, Sunday evening BTU. Whether we believed in God or not didn't matter. Our people did, so we spent a lifetime trying to please Him.

At church we learned how to pray, how to approach the "throne of Grace." God was not to be handled clumsily; one had to know the verbiage, the vernacular rhythm necessary to speak to an almighty, omniscient God. Usually children weren't called upon to pray, except on special occasions like Youth Day. Then, parents and elders smiled and listened as youngsters fumbled their way through rehearsed church jargon, trying as best they could to mimic the vernacular of their folks. It was always a far cry from what the deacons or mothers could do. When they prayed, the angels and cherubim stood still. These old black folks would bow to their knees, before a plain wooden chair, and begin, "God of Abraham, Isaac, and Jacob. God of yesterday, today, and forevermore. We beseech Thee, oh God, to hear our prayers and supplications. We magnify You, oh God, and glorify You, and exalt You high! You are the keeper and the healer of our souls!" Or something like that. I'm a grown man and still I can't pray like those elders. It was an art, a soul's desperate, poetic plea. Some of the language came from the Bible itself. They never used words like "supplication" or "beseech" in everyday speech. But I suppose it made sense to think that God liked those expressions since He'd used them in His book. That, of course, is another story.

The black church is the oldest social institution black people own and operate. Founded during the antebellum period, it began in hush harbors—those "steal away" places in the forest, next to rivers and streams, where water absorbed the sound of prayers and music and thick foliage shielded desperate black believers. Yes, there are other black institutions—the Nation of Islam, independent black schools, the Nation of Ndugu and Nzinga—but none share the historical impact of the black church on black social and political progress. Indeed, over the years, the black church has kept black people alive. Literally. It has provided space in which to meet, pray, strategize, and even sleep sometimes. In its inception, it gave poor, disenfranchised black people imaginative context wherein to construct identity and communal value. These marginalized human beings became somebody on Sunday mornings when they morphed into Sunday school teachers, deacons, ushers, and choir soloists. For hundreds of years, maids and janitors, mechanics and cooks, gathered in black sanctuaries, believing that God had something special reserved for the poor yet unwavering. Cloaked in Sunday-best frocks, black folks strutted to church and poured their hearts out to God, pleading for miracles they could only imagine. My family was among them. We went to church every Sunday in rural Arkansas—

absolutely every single Sunday. No excuses. Even when we weren't feeling well, we pressed our way. I recall being nauseated one Sunday morning, and Daddy telling me, "Grab a trash bag and let's go."

All communal events happened at the church—family reunions, picnics, baby showers, funerals—and everyone assisted in its maintenance. Every few months, families gathered and cleaned it as if preparing for God's arrival. Men and boys did the external labor, mowing grass or trimming trees or painting, while women and girls dusted pews, swept, and cleaned the kitchen. A shabby church was a disgrace to a people. Elders voiced harsh criticism for those communities in which churches appeared dilapidated and uncared for. The church was our collective achievement, our pride on display, and we meant to show the world who we were.

The problem, of course, is that we couldn't clean the theology. Most of our preachers and pastors had no more learning than the average congregant, so they spewed the same destructive rhetoric slave masters taught a century before. "We are nothing but filthy rags before a perfect savior," I recall Pastor saying one morning. I frowned. I knew I had faults, but was I a *filthy rag*?

Another time, he said, "I wouldn't mind being a slave if Jesus is my master!" Again, my eyes bulged. I didn't want to be anybody's slave. I thought we had gotten past that. And of course he didn't believe women should preach. Most black people, unfortunately, agreed. In fact, he read scriptures that limited women's influence both in the church and the home. None of this made sense to me. Most black women I knew ran their homes with fierce strength and efficiency. Certainly men couldn't do it, so why would we as a people follow that instruction? That's when I began to believe we'd been reading a book meant for another people. I didn't say that then though.

But I'm saying it now. The downfall of the black church is that it keeps teaching its own bondage. We can't seem to find the courage to disagree with scripture or, more powerfully, articulate new ideas that contradict what we were once told. We fear the Christian God the same way we feared slave captors. If we're not careful, we'll discover the two as one and the same.

Black theologians have been urging black people for years to reconstruct our own notions of God, Heaven, the Bible, and spirituality in general. James Cone, Renita Weems, Jacquelyn Grant, Howard Thurman, Kelly Brown Douglas, Catherine Meeks, and so many more challenge contemporary black churches to renegotiate our understanding of God and our relationship to divinity. For example, Kelly Brown Douglas's *Sexuality and the Black Church* upends traditional black beliefs about God's view of sexuality and, in fact, invites black people to dismiss the Eurocentric idea that sexual fluidity is not divine. These are the radical considerations that would make the modern black church relevant and attractive to a new generation of congregants. Yet, for some reason, these liberative ideas get modified before they reach most black pulpits. This has cost the black church dearly. It's as if many black pastors fear the wrath of a ubiquitous, tyrannical, (white) God if they dare say anything that goes against traditional Christian ideals. Because of this, the black church has, in many ways, imprisoned its own people. It's taught black versions of white supremacist thinking and celebrated itself for the rejection of pagan, Africanist ways. There are black churches today that frown upon or straight out deny the legitimacy of African rituals such as libation in the sanctuary. Many contend that honoring ancestors is downright demonic. They often adhere to the Western belief that African traditional practices are "heathenish" and "evil," meaning full of witchcraft and sorcery. This, then, means that they never consult Africa or African culture as the source of a new, black spirituality. Rather, many black churches—far too many—depend upon Eurocentric understandings of God and spirit in ways that make them hate themselves.

Take, for instance, the tradition of posting white images of Christ in black sanctuaries. I have questioned this insanity for years, only to be told, time and again, that "Jesus's color doesn't matter."

"If that's true," I ask, "why is he usually white?" Have you ever seen a black image of Christ in a white church? I haven't. You know why? Because most whites won't worship a black savior. They might vote for a black president, but following a black man into eternity is another matter. Most blacks won't either. Nonetheless, the point is that the color of Christ *does* matter, and, in fact, one's ability to conceive of himself/herself *as* Christ is spirituality made perfect. The identity of the historical Christ is, for the most part, irrelevant because Christ is far more imagined than real; so if that imagining does not reflect a people's own cultural Self, those people's self-worth is seriously impaired.

Let me return to the notion that "slaves should obey their masters." 1 Peter 2:18 says specifically, "Slaves, be subject to your masters with all reverence, not only to those who are good and equitable but also to those who are perverse." What the hell? Are black people not thinking? Who would teach this as the Word of God? Some will argue for the legitimacy of this scripture in context, but there is *no context* to make this idea holy. Even understanding one's self as God's slave is problematic because then God gets authority to treat people without respect and dignity. And let me say for the record that if God wants slaves, I don't want God. Plus, such a paradigm is dangerous for people who just completed four hundred years of captivity. I know the mandate that one is not supposed to change the Word of God, but that's part of the problem—understanding the Bible as the *only* Word of God. How ironic that the descendants of slaves worship the same book, in much the same way, as those who enslaved them! This is the text that justified, and continues to justify, their brutalization. It should at least be scrutinized and amended, shouldn't it?

I have a better idea. Let's sanction some black-authored works as the Word of God. Let's believe that we, too, can write holy scripture that articulates God's heart. Anything less is insulting and self-rejecting. Let's take the pulpit next Sunday and read from, say, *The Bluest Eye*. Pecola's story is just as healing, just as immaculate, as Mary's. Or let's study *The Color Purple* and see how patriarchy destroys an entire nation. This is black agency in action. Or if you want a story of a savior and his resurrection, read Ernest Gaines's *A Lesson Before Dying*. God's character in black permeates that narrative and teaches self-love in its purest form. For black people *not* to refer to their own literary tradition when they search for the Word of God is quintessential self-hatred. There are other texts too—*The Fire Next Time*, *The Souls of Black Folk*, *Jesus and the Disinherited*, *Two Thousand Seasons*, *Kindred*, and, more contemporarily, Jericho Brown's *The Tradition*, Kiese Laymon's *Heavy*, Jesmyn Ward's *Sing, Unburied, Sing*, Edwidge Danticat's *The Farm-*

ing of Bones. The black pen never fails to produce spirit-filled work that, if black people read and heed, would set them free. Black people in churches all across America would shout with deliverance and revelation if their souls were fed this discursive delight on Sunday morning. We hear God as clearly as any other people on this planet. We can speak for God, too.

Concerning women, we should be ashamed of the ubiquitous patriarchy in the black church. Black women pay bills, cook, clean, instruct, and prophesy at home, then get to church and are told to sit down and be quiet? This makes no sense at all, even if the Bible mandates it. Our mothers and sisters have led liberation struggles, guided black men to freedom, run for president of the United States (before any man), and devised mathematical equations to get a person to the moon and back. But they can't preach? I understand Jarena Lee's fury. She said, "If the man may preach, because the Savior died for him, why not the woman, seeing he died for her also? Is he not a whole Savior, instead of half of one?" Her theology was in her body—not just a book. She knew God—not just the story of a Christ. And she undoubtedly expected black men to understand since they shared her history of discrimination. But they didn't. Still, she pressed on and preached anyway. There must've been days when, as a black woman, she spoke to an audience of only one or two listeners. She might've even preached to the trees and animals of the forest. She probably didn't mind. She wanted to share God's word and didn't care with whom she shared it.

Those who wrote the Bible didn't know the history of black women. They didn't understand that black women paid the same cost as black men for black people's liberty. They didn't know that black women birthed children and chopped cotton all in the same day. They didn't know that black women breastfed their enemies' children then breastfed their own. They couldn't have known the torture of rape and sexual assault black women endured daily while smiling and fighting to maintain a home. Writers of the Bible surely never saw a woman run like Harriet Tubman or dance like Katherine Dunham. If they had, they would've known that, for black people, God is a woman too. The Maroons of Jamaica would have died without Nanny's strength and leadership; the Montgomery Bus Boycott would never have happened without the organizational brilliance of Jo Ann Robinson and the Women's Political Council; Barack Obama would never have ascended to the White House except for a brilliant, savvy black woman named Shirley Chisholm, who paved his way, and a priceless, genius black woman named Michelle, who guided and shielded him. In truth, it's insulting, now, to hear black churches teach misogynistic articles of Western submission *after* black women have stood at the vanguard of history and defended our communities with their lives. This is madness! Yes, we need to revise the Bible—or, better, get busy writing our own. This is real liberation. God will not be offended. Indeed, God might be proud that, finally, black people assume themselves divine, too.

At thirteen, I witnessed a horror in the church that shaped my sensitivity to black women. A teenage girl—we'll call her Sarah—got pregnant out of wedlock. She was sixteen, and a member of our church. One Sunday, before the sermon, Sarah came forward, trembling like a newborn calf, prepared to "beg the church's pardon." This was a moment when unmarried pregnant girls apologized to the congregation for the "stain" of their sin. My eyes bulged with terror. I'd never witnessed this before, never heard of such a thing, but there it was. And Sarah had to do it or else be dismissed from the church. So she stood alone, weeping the while, as her parents and the congregation stared in repulsive judgment. "I just want to say," she murmured, "that I'm sorry for what I did." Tears fell onto the red carpet beneath her. Sarah never lifted her head. "I didn't mean to bring shame to the house of God. I wanna ask y'all to forgive me—" her voice broke "—for being outside of God's will. And I wanna stay in the church if y'all will have me." I looked around in bewilderment, wondering who had required such public disgrace, only to discover that everyone supported this shaming process. I shook my head slowly and cried for her. The congregation's gaze softened once she finished, but, by then, I hated the church.

Later, Daddy confronted me about my facial expression during the ordeal. "You got somethin' to say 'bout that girl comin' befo the church today?" he asked, threateningly. Of course I had something to say, but I wasn't bold enough to say it. Instead, I asked, "Is the boy comin' too?" Daddy's eyes narrowed with rage. "Boys don't get pregnant." That's when I risked sayin', "I know, but they get girls pregnant, so what's the difference? It's at least half his fault." I was prepared to be slapped in the mouth, yet Daddy sighed and told me to mind my own business, so I did. But I didn't agree. I imagined my sister standing there, seeking forgiveness from people who had no holiness to boast of, and I knew I wouldn't have allowed her to stand alone, even if it meant leaving the church altogether. I'm still ashamed I didn't stand with Sarah that day. Hopefully, she'll read this and know that I wanted to.

It's taken me years to survive the memory of that travesty.

Sarah probably never did. She had the baby and stayed in the church, undoubtedly because she had no other choice, no other place to go. She was the last girl I saw endure that torture, so I believed the church discovered the error of its ways. Otherwise, I would've left it entirely. At least I think I would've.

My struggle was that I loved the same institution I hated. Still do. Its music soothes my soul when nothing else can. There is no sound in the world like black church music. So many serious African American vocalists were trained in the church. Aretha Franklin, Sam Cooke, Gladys Knight, Yolanda Adams, James Cleveland, Quincy Jones, Mahalia Jackson, Kirk Franklin. Too many to number. The black church is keeper of the black aesthetic, storehouse of black rhythmic expression, home of musical interpretations of black pain and triumph. The church was, until integration, the only place wherein black pathos went uncontested. It existed outside the imposing white gaze and offered clandestine space for the birthing of black spiritual and intellectual thought. Black people were free, or at least *freer,* there than any other place in the world. That's why I loved it. The shouting and crying and moaning and dancing and singing were a healing balm for me. Outside the church, people didn't hug me or love me quite so earnestly. But something about the church gave them permission to do so, and I needed the affirmation badly. I was a creative, musical, sensitive black boy—a dangerous combination in the black community—yet the church became my stage. I recited poems for Easter and Christmas with precisely the drama people enjoyed, and they praised me for it. I sang in the choir, and once I started piano lessons, I became the church musician, ushering in spirit in ways that felt natural and empowering. I needed the church, for without it, I would've been little more than a desperate, artistic black boy who had no social value at all.

Through gospel music, I discovered the depth of my emotions. I could cry freely when I sang, and no one reprimanded me. Often, others cried along as I belted notes of my favorite songs. Hymns like "The Lord Will Make a Way Somehow" and "Oh I Want To See Him" convinced me that, as others whispered about my femininity, I would survive because God loved me even if they didn't. This might sound desperate, but it's where I was at the time. I took the lyrics literally. In other songs, I clung onto metaphors of power and resistance that left me encouraged. One famous hymn of the church says, "Pass me not, oh gentle Savior! Hear my humble cry! While on others Thou art calling, do not pass me by." I imagined myself standing among a crowd of anxious believers, reaching and grasping for Jesus's hand, only to be pushed aside and overlooked. Yet, somehow, Jesus found me, lingering at the margins, and gathered me into his arms as if I were his own.

The song always touched me deeply. I needed that touch, too, because, at thirteen or so, I wrestled demons too powerful to conquer. My mother had abandoned my brother and me as babies, and we never knew why. Each of us processed it differently: I hid behind books; he shut down emotionally. And, to make matters worse, my father wouldn't speak of her. He wanted to erase her memory, to forget that she ever existed. So my brother and I struggled to feel wanted. When time came for me to date, I had no desire to do so. Looking back now, I think I felt unworthy and unattractive. What I wanted most was to run away, but there was nowhere to go. I'm not sure I had the courage to do it anyway. So I sat in the center of Arkansas, begging God to love me and cover me until I could leave. I had no sense of personal agency, no confidence that anyone cared what I thought, so I shut up and waited. I think a lot of black kids did. We were taught that silence was golden and that children's opinions meant nothing to grown people. And since adults had very little to say to me, I tried to discern the message in their whisperings, which was often unkind and, sometimes, downright mean. So church songs became my refuge, promising the coming of a perfect Savior who would, one day, usher me into paradise. This hope calmed my turbulent spirit and assured me that, somehow, I'd live and not die.

One song in particular carried me the distance. It was released in 1975 on an album titled *Love Alive*. I was just a kid, already playing for the church, but when I heard this song, I sat on the floor and sobbed. It came on the radio late one night, when R & B stations switched over to gospel. The announcer said the artist was a guy named Walter Hawkins, but the soloist was his wife, Tramaine. The song was titled, very simply, "Changed." She belted, "A wonderful change has come over me. He changed my life and now I'm free." All I could do was shiver. I had wanted, all my young life, for God to change me into something acceptable, something laudable, which others would praise and celebrate. I had prayed—no, I had begged and pleaded—for God to do something transformative with me that would erase all the things others said God didn't like about me. This song suggested that God would do it—if I would "work and work until He comes." So I fell to my knees and committed to a life of piety, free of things folks said God didn't like such as sex, drinking, drugs, and violence. And I upheld the commitment. I didn't have sex or taste alcohol until my midtwenties. I am not ashamed of this.

I had entered a covenant with God, and if God was willing to change me, I was willing to sacrifice everything for it.

But God didn't change me.

So I drowned in gospel music for the next ten years. These songs helped me imagine a world where everyone was free and loved and admired for who they were. This was the 1980s, the black gospel choir movement years, and every time I heard a choir scream from the depths of their souls, I lifted my hands in praise. The loud, cacophonous sounds of multiple black voices in harmony excited me because it's precisely the way I understood community. I loved a God who had the capacity to love the entire world. I understood those brash, shouting, screeching tones as a collective desire for God to do what our elders had promised He would do—save us, heal us, deliver us. Gospel choirs across the nation became famous for songs that kept black people from destroying themselves and others: Milton Brunson and the Thompson Community Singers—"There Is No Failure in God"; James Cleveland and the Angelic Choir—"Peace Be Still"; the LA Mass Choir—"That's When You Bless Me"; Thomas Whitfield and the Thomas Whitfield Company—"I Shall Wear a Crown"; The Edwin Hawkins Singers—"Oh Happy Day." These songs articulated black angst and black hope in ways that made sense to me. They convinced me that my suffering, and, by extension, black suffering, wasn't a fruitless endeavor.

The black church was once good for something else, too. Back in the day, it provided the platform upon which black children learned the art of public speaking. We took this for granted, and surely underestimated its import, but Easter and Christmas speeches planted seeds of confidence and authority in black children from whom the world expected very little.

From age two, children were forced—and I do mean *forced*—to stand before congregations of black elders as they recited poems or song lyrics until the people found their delivery acceptable. Children were not allowed to whisper or bow their heads in shame; quite the antithesis, youth leaders—every black church had one—drilled kids until they spoke with pride and boldness. Tears did not free a child from this requirement. Indeed, tears often solicited a switch or belt across a child's backside. I didn't understand this then, but I do now. Black people knew the dangers of rearing insecure black children. They understood well that if one could not speak up on their own behalf, their future was in peril. The black community could not afford to breed squeamish, fragile, timid youth who would not challenge power structures. Black life was a perpetual battle, which the reticent were sure to lose. The only way to win, even occasionally, was to be stalwart and confrontational in the face of discrimination and inequality. Black children would not survive, black elders believed, if they couldn't hold their heads high and speak clearly and courageously. This was the point of making children read scriptures aloud and forcing them to speak on youth days. Speeches lengthened as children aged, so high school students sometimes memorized whole pages of texts. This is the rhetorical foundation of famous public speakers like Martin Luther King Jr., Jesse Jackson, Al Sharpton, Fannie Lou Hamer, Sojourner Truth, Jarena Lee, Frederick Douglass, and practically every other leader the black community has ever known. Against America's belief, black rhetorical excellence sprouted and bore its finest fruit in the black church. Children learned the value and convictions of black people while standing before them on Sunday mornings. They were not unclear about what it meant to "carry one's self with dignity" or to "walk upright." These phrases meant something very specific, and the strength to speak publicly was part of it. Black sanctuaries gave children space and permission to "open their mouths" and be somebody.

One of my fondest childhood memories was Youth Day 1980. I was fifteen and old enough to get a "big kids" speech. Yet our youth leader—we'll call her Miss Irene—had a surprise in store for me. Weeks before the event, she handed me an envelope and, without smiling or asking me anything, said, "Here you go, young man. Learn every word of it. Do not fumble, stumble, or hesitate." Then she walked away. I knew better than complaining to my parents; they agreed with her. All elders agreed in our community when it came to children. I didn't open the envelope until I got home. When I saw what she had given me to memorize, I whispered, intensely, "Shit." I had no choice. I had to do it. And I had to do it well, or else I'd be in all kinds of trouble. Miss Irene knew the kind of student I was—she'd asked about my grades since elementary school—so I got busy learning the speech and trying to contort my tenor voice to a deeper baritone.

It took me weeks to memorize that speech. I carried it with me everywhere—the hay barn, the pea patch, geometry class—and kids laughed at me, mumbling throughout the day, trying to sound like Martin Luther King Jr. I ignored their jeering. I had a mission to accomplish, a self-worth to prove. Daddy joked one morning at the breakfast table: "She got you good this time, huh?" I shook my head, but I didn't intend to fail.

When the day came, I wore a brand-new baby blue short-sleeved shirt. I didn't really care for blue, but I looked good in it, and that was the point. One by one, Miss Irene called children forward and they performed their respective speeches. I wasn't the oldest, but she left me for last. I knew why. Everyone else did, too.

Finally, she rose and said emphatically, "Now!" pausing as if preparing people for the inconceivable. I closed my eyes and exhaled. Sweat streamed from my temples and fell upon my pretty blue shirt, leaving navy blue splotches. Yet I had come too far to give up. So after Miss Irene boasted of my stellar grades and declared that I'd be a doctor someday, I rose and stood before the podium, just below the pulpit. Only preachers spoke from the pulpit.

I said nothing introductory. I simply took a deep breath, glanced across the audience, and began in a bold, loud voice: "I am happy to join with you today in what will go down in history as the greatest demonstration for freedom in the history of our nation!" One deacon said, "Come on, boy!" so I continued: "Five score years ago, a great American in whose symbolic shadow we stand today signed the Emancipation Proclamation." I overarticulated the last two words, the way I'd heard preachers do with scripture, and the crowd pounced to their feet.

"That's what I'm talkin' 'bout!"

"Listen here!"

"That boy gon change the world! You watch!"

That was the affirmation I needed. Even Daddy nodded, which was more praise than he usually gave anyone. Miss Irene rocked side to side like she did when the Holy Ghost overwhelmed her.

I moved through the entire speech, emphasizing words and phrases I knew would touch my people and whispering in places that caused a few to weep. When I got to the last line,

I stepped away from the podium and raised my arms as if raising the dead, and bellowed, "Free at last, free at last, great God a-mighty, we are free at last!" I stared at the ceiling, waiting for God and the angels to burst forth. The applause deafened. Some shouted and danced. Miss Irene wiped tears and rubbed her thick arms. I felt seen that day. Kids told me later, "Man, that was incredible! You set the house on fire! You memorized *all of that*?" I nodded proudly. But I was not exceptional. I was the fruit of what my people believed—that, if you stand up straight and open yo mouth, God will speak for you. Then the world will have no choice but to listen.

However, somewhere along the way, the black church traded social consciousness for respectability politics. It had always been an institution governed by standards of public decency, but by the '80s, it became the undisputed center of black decorum and propriety. Churches were unapologetic, for example, about sending a girl home if, say, her skirt was too short. If they didn't send her home, they would lay a scarf or sweater across her lap as an act of modesty. This bred shame and humiliation, although black people meant to establish and maintain a standard of public dignity. It affected boys, too. Before the 1980s—yes, *that* recently—many black churches wouldn't allow boys to wear earrings or braided hair in the sanctuary. The problem with these edicts is that they served ultimately to keep black people "presentable" before white eyes. This is complicated, certainly, as part of the aim was the maintenance of appropriate appearance, which, to many, translated into black employability. Yet, on the other hand, this policing of black bodies was the adoption of Eurocentric standards by which black people would judge and govern themselves. Said another way, the black church used white cultural values as its focal referent, its model of what a strong, powerful religious institution might look like.

This backfired in the '80s and '90s. Post-integration black youth critiqued the church in ways their parents had never considered. Black children of that era voted against the policing of their self-expression and argued for the inclusion of their voices in policy-making matters. I was one of those youth who loved the church but despised its politics. Everything fun was sinful—movies, drinking, dance clubs, sex—although we knew elders who partook in all of these. Some of them had children out of wedlock, too. Or children by different spouses. The contradictions were endless and infuriating, so we began to speak our minds. That didn't always go well. Sometimes, in the face of opposition, youth simply left. This confirmed to many that the black church had no space for a new black generation, one uncommitted to old standards of choking piety and silent self-righteousness.

The bottom line is that the black church needs an overhaul. It's stuck in its own mire of tradition and indiscernible love of white supremacy. It has limited God only to what Christians perceive, and it has all but disconnected itself from the ideology and radical nature of its founders. It also needs desperately to follow the advice of contemporary black theologians and eradicate gender hierarchies such that even the question of whether women can or cannot preach becomes laughable. We need a black church that isn't afraid to play hip-hop in the sanctuary—cuss words and all—both for critique and praise of lyrics that might liberate the saints. We need a church that celebrates SGL (same-gender-loving) members and is honored to host their weddings. We need a church where a black image of Christ welcomes parishioners on Sunday mornings without folks wondering what white people think about it. We need a new Jerusalem! Better yet, a new Kemet!

But ultimately, we need the black church. Its influence was once unmatched, such that it saved an entire people. The civil rights movement was made possible because of the black church. It was the keeper, the protector, the spiritual fortress of the 1950s/1960s social crusade for human rights. Marchers organized in the church; peace strategists argued in the church; freedom riders slept in the church; boycotts were sustained by the church; leaders met and prayed in the church; rallies were held in the church; money was raised in the church; children learned nonviolent tactics in the church; slain leaders were laid to rest in the church—everything the movement needed happened in the church. Even the music of the church framed the ethos of the times. A radical social justice agenda was born and bred in the 1960s black church, a reality that assured that civil rights would one day be realized. Black people became one voice in the church and advocated for the transformation of the entire world.

Another priceless social function of the black church, especially in rural areas, was its dual role as sanctuary and classroom. Down in the country, the church was the school. Literally. This is a powerful metaphor, as poor, black, country folks replaced pews and pulpits on Sunday evening with desks and blackboards on Monday morning. At week's end, this transformation was reversed, and the church restored. This symbiotic relationship between knowledge and spirit exposes black people's belief, at least prior to the 1970s, that only God and education could save us. It also suggests that, in some ways, black folks recognize knowledge *as* spirit. The point of learning was the creation of a better being, a more righteous life—not simply the acquisition of money or material things. Black people wanted a changed world, so tending their spirit and mind in the same place made sound existential sense. Yet this symbiosis dissolved after the 1960s, when black schools and black churches parted ways, and neither has been the better for it.

After the 1970s, the black church moved away from grassroots concerns to an obsession with Heaven alone. Perhaps the traumatic assassinations of Malcolm, Medgar, and Martin convinced black folks that earth offered no real, tangible hope of human gain; therefore, the only thing worth living for was the afterlife. If this broader shift truly occurred, and I believe it did, it means the black church surrendered its position as the gatekeeper of justice. It relinquished its long-held status as the Home of the Ancestors, the mouthpiece of the marginalized, the spiritual fortress that speaks truth to those in power regardless of the outcome. The real effect was that the more "like Christ" we became, the more neglectful of our own social condition we also became. I wondered why, for example, the black church didn't respond to the ways corporate moguls literally bought black children's voices during the birth of hip-hop. Few have written about this tragedy, but as our primary social institution, the black church should've been on the vanguard around what black youth say and sing about, especially in exchange for millions of dollars. This reeks of the auction block all over again except, this time, it's the black voice white America paid so dearly for. The result has practically devastated black people. We rap our own demise and think nothing of it. Of course there are brilliant, talented, positive-speaking hip-hop artists such as Common,

Tobe Nwigwe, Talib Kweli, and Oddisee. Yet I argue that America exalts the self-deprecating black artist because, ultimately, this reifies the allure of white supremacy. Nonetheless, my point is that I had thought (I had hoped) the black church would've fought harder to protect the sanctity of black youth's voices. Most churches, I'm afraid, were too busy exalting an already exalted Christ. Black children felt this neglect and wondered what it meant to have elders who would die for Jesus but not for them. They've never gotten over it. Some of the vulgarity in the music is their response.

In the '80s and '90s, the black church response to HIV/AIDS was equally abysmal. Some churches had AIDS ministries and prayer groups, but few stomped the streets to protest how AIDS patients were treated. And even fewer churches reconsidered their position on gays and lesbians since their lives were on the line. Instead, many black churches said AIDS was the wrath of God upon homosexuals. This sounds unintelligent now—it was unintelligent then—but twenty-five years ago, most black churches were so anti-gay that they used the disease to justify their public condemnation of LGBTQ congregants. "God hates sin!" I heard one preacher announce happily. "And sooner or later He's gonna do something about it. Like this whole AIDS thing. Don't you see the hand of God in this, cleaning up what folks done messed up?" I bowed my head. I wasn't bold enough to object out loud because too many people agreed with him. The "amens" and "shonuffs" convinced me to keep my mouth shut. People were already suspicious of my presence among that crowd, so I sat silently as church after church blamed gay people for dying because they refused to deny each other their bodies. This is saddest because these same people carried the ethos of the church.

They were the musicians, choir directors, soloists, and praise dancers without whom the church would've had no spirit at all. To use these people's gifts while simultaneously condemning their nature was and is disrespect most egregious. And taking their money while sending them to Hell is an unforgivable contradiction. This is why so many black youths, in the '90s, left the church. The contradictions, the insensitive judgment, the demeaning of people's authentic self was more than a new, integrated generation could tolerate. The inability of the church to recognize AIDS as a social dilemma and a medical epidemic caused countless black people to kiss the church goodbye.

Even worse, many black churches wouldn't bury those who died from AIDS. They were memorialized at funeral chapels in near-silent services that never acknowledged these people's contribution to the church. Often, preachers wouldn't admit that these brothers and sisters even had AIDS. They called it "cancer" or "pneumonia" or nothing at all. Worse still, there was almost never a viewing. People were downright ashamed of what these young people looked like, so they refused to bear any embarrassment for them. Far too often, black church leaders sanctioned this behavior. Sometimes they initiated it.

In other instances, the church sponsored all-night prayer services for those who wanted to rid themselves of the homosexual demon. Yet there were not all-night deliverance services for alcoholics and those with children by multiple partners. No other "sin" was treated with such disgust and contempt. A few churches did AIDS outreach and held HIV seminars, but almost none collected money for HIV research. Or embraced gay people and their identity as part of the kingdom of God. Black conservatives argued that we shouldn't expect the church to do this because, as an institution, it doesn't believe in homosexuality and thus has every right to condemn it. Perhaps this is true. But what it doesn't have the right to do is use the life force of gay people and treat them like trash. That, my friend, can't be right.

More recently, the black church has also proven essentially useless regarding the senseless killings of young black men and women. I don't mean that churches haven't mentioned this reality or even prayed about it; I mean that few black churches, as a unified body, have confronted power structures and demanded change. The average American citizen sits in anger and wonders what they can do. The church seems similarly paralyzed. This is the problem—the fact that the black church has lost much of its imaginative potency. It once possessed a social consciousness that allowed it to create solutions to crises that threatened black life. Now it takes refuge in prayer alone. But before I'm misunderstood, let me say clearly that prayer has power; prayer *is* power. We need it, for prayer fights battles in invisible places our bodies can't go. We simply need it alongside human action. We gotta pray *and* stomp the streets for justice *and* send letters to Congress *and* confront police precincts with our collective force. We might need to do this instead of meeting on Sunday morning, for this is spirituality in action. However, too many church folks, along with the rest of the world, shake their heads and hope that *somebody* does *something* about the murder of our people.

Many black youths, especially of the revolutionary sort, find this safety, this socially devoid gospel, repugnant. So they've left the church. And this isn't a few people; it's practically an entire generation. Scholars and journalists alike have, in the last several years, written about the trend of black (and white) millennials and Generation Zers to abandon organized religion. I contend that this trend started in the '70s when integration and compulsory education made knowledge accessible to black kids in ways it had never been before. This meant that black youth were using new analytical skills that invited their critique of traditional black church customs and mores. They made (and still make) claims against the church in terms of patriarchy, misogyny, homophobia, classism, and the like. They found (and find) the "pie in the sky" mentality socially irresponsible. Their collective mantra is "When Heaven becomes the reason we don't do anything, I don't wanna go there." Eventually, black youth gained enough knowledge and spiritual gall to challenge the church's antiquated beliefs and policies. This tension persists unto today. Contemporary youth, for instance, decry the church's rejection and/or suppression of queer and women's voices. They find this behavior ignorant and spiritually indefensible. They don't agree, and they don't think God agrees. Most significantly, they hate that the church lags far behind the general society in terms of acceptance and celebration of difference. In fact, many laugh in scorn as these institutions struggle with issues young people find silly and irrelevant. Some youth are exploring other spiritual systems—Ifá, Buddhism, Santeria—that free them from the stilted confines of the black church. This means that, if the black church isn't careful, its days are numbered.

Yet the dismantling of the black church would devastate the black community. Social institutions do mighty—and sometimes invisible—work for people, like providing spaces for important gatherings and serving as the epicenter of a people's collective identity and heritage. Indeed, the black church has been the social memory of black people since our forced arrival. Without it, we would've had nowhere to go and nowhere to hide. Now, in this modern hour, we don't yet have sufficient institutional options such that we can afford to lose the church. Too much of our history, our collective character, our aesthetic power dwells in it for us to abandon it altogether. However, without an immediate reconstruction of policy, theology, and social consciousness, that's precisely what young black people are prepared—*and willing*—to do.

BLACK, BUT NOT BEAUTIFUL: AN AESTHETIC DILEMMA

One of the vestiges of American slavery is black people's belief in our own ugliness. This was no accident. Color bias was systematically constructed on early plantations and perpetuated throughout the antebellum period via folklore, newspapers, skewed scientific data, and ever-popular minstrel shows. Europeans worked hard to associate the color black with evil, debauchery, and devilish behavior while exalting whiteness as divine, pure, and supreme. Even today, countless cultural artifacts preserve this deadly idea: Angel food cake is white, while devil's food cake is black; white is the color of weddings, while black is for funerals; God is always cloaked in white, while witches and wizards don black robes. The list goes on and on.

Such signifiers teach the erroneous notion that whiteness is inherently supreme, and blackness is, by definition, unruly, undesirable, and unholy. Over time, African descendants bought into this foolishness because the paucity of our material lives seemingly upheld European assertions of black inferiority. After all, we worked as hard as anyone, but, for whatever reason, did not collectively prosper. So the illogical notion of black inferiority became believable.

This idea has decimated black life for four hundred years. Many—I daresay most—African Americans still struggle with the notion of their physical beauty. They might not think of themselves as downright ugly, but they envy attractive people the way the poor envy the rich. This aesthetic inheritance is not easily shaken. Black self-loathing today takes many forms: drug and sex addictions, violence, poor health maintenance, hair obsession. Magazine images, television sitcoms, and popular movies still reinforce America's belief that anything black is unpleasant, and, in fact, threatening. From the moment of capture till now, black people have endured daily reminders that their physical features are reprehensible. Slave masters, teachers, bus drivers, and, yes, even parents have declared, "You're too dark," "Your nose is too broad," "You got some flat feet," "Your hair is nappy," "Your lips are thick," "Your butt is huge," "You got a big forehead." Most black children can speak of the horror of these declarations and, often, later in life, explain their impact on their self-esteem. If they can't connect the two, their behavior usually does.

In the early years of captivity, enslaved people learned to reject African features and thus discovered their bodies as the source of their bondage. Said differently, I believe they associated their abhorrent social condition with their physical characteristics and thus, over time, grew to believe that their looks contributed to their confinement. This overcritiquing and condemnation of the black body led many blacks to participate in the cultural practice of paralleling African traits with black delinquency. Hence, it's no surprise that today, corporate America frowns upon locks and braids as the opposite of "professional attire," and many Americans still interpret broad noses and big lips as signs of aggression. Ironically, the black people white folks deemed most beautiful looked *least* like the others. In other words, black beauty was most achievable if one's blood was infused with someone else's blood. "I have Indian in me," too many black people state with great pride. In some cases, those with "good hair" or "soft, curly hair" or "wavy, loose hair" were prized and sought after as people who favored God. I remember this well. In the '70s, anyone light-skinned was cute simply because of their complexion—not their actual features. A friend once spoke of a girl as pretty, and I said, "She's not cute at all!" and he said, "Sure she is! Don't you see that redbone complexion?"

Some might think this changed over time. Indeed, the 2000s ushered in an era when dark-skinned black men (especially) were in vogue. But it was culturally disingenuous. Yes, being dark became fetishized, but that's not the same as a revolution in self-consciousness. See, the darkness people now crave is a black *with miscegenational features*. It's dark skin with narrow noses and cute, almond-shaped eyes—Idris Elba, Morris Chestnut, Chadwick Boseman, Tyson Beckford—not dark skin cloaking traditional African characteristics. For instance, few people ever speak of Leslie Jones as gorgeous or a heartthrob. Lupita Nyong'o makes the cut because she's dark *and* thin and pretty in an American sort of way. She just *happens* to be dark also. Even Djimon Hounsou fits the bill because, although his forehead is big, his lips and eyes are not so large as to be frightening. This is Daniel Kaluuya's aesthetic shortfall seemingly. His complexion meets the standard of sexy darkness, but his bulbous eyes supposedly betray him. They don't suggest humility to a Eurocentric gaze; they imply disobedience and rage, and America has had enough of that.

I googled "black male heartthrobs" and "sexy black men" and these names appeared: Shemar Moore, Blair Underwood, Laz Alonso, Boris Kodjoe, Michael Ealy, Tyrese Gibson, Lamman Rucker, etc. And these brothers *are* fine. No argument about that. But the problem is that they tend to share similar features. And most of these features are not African-aesthetic based. Why is this a problem? Because, then, most black male aesthetic heroes don't favor the men they're supposed to represent. Consequently, the average black man understands himself as "lacking" and "wanting" in physical desirability and therefore looks for other ways to have meaning in a world that values him only for his body. "Regular" black men then use money, alcohol, and other external mechanisms to endure while hoping someone will, one day, want them.

The same is true for black women. When I googled "gorgeous black women" and "black women heartthrobs", these names appeared: Jada Pinkett Smith, Janet Jackson, Taraji P. Henson, Sanaa Lathan, Rihanna, Kerry Washington, Janelle Monáe, Beyoncé, etc. Again, unmistakably beautiful black women, but those who tend to share similar facial traits. I wondered why they didn't list Viola Davis—immeasurably beautiful—then I admitted the answer: Her characteristics are not as *humble* as the others'. She carries the skin tone, lips, eyes, and nose that make others believe she could evolve into the angry black woman in seconds. Also, for those who do see her as attractive, I fear it's more out of fetish than actual desirability. In other words, she's pretty "for a dark-skinned black woman" as I've heard many say. This is an old aphorism, a terse noncomplimentary statement that exposes one's *surprise* that beauty *could* rest upon such an undesirable black face. And, to be sure, black women's aesthetic burden is arguably heavier than black men's since their bodies have been used disproportionately, from America's beginning, to service both white male pleasure and American economic interests. Black women's aesthetic presentation has determined their quality of life since their arrival in the New World. Today, their presence in music videos, strip clubs, Hollywood movies, and magazines reifies the fight to recast the image of black women as substantively more than the source of men's appetites. Yet, often, this appetite makes black girls long for the hope of aesthetic value and hence judge themselves against the images of black women they see most often—all too few of whom look like themselves.

The consequences of this dilemma have deteriorated the foundation of the black community. This subconscious self-loathing makes romantic relationships almost impossible to sustain. Why? Because many black people spend a lifetime running after and hoping for association with *the beautiful ones.* This means that even when regular, moderately attractive people connect, their dream is unsatisfied, their real desire unachieved. The real problem, as aforementioned, is a subconscious belief in one's own ugliness. In 1970, Toni Morrison released a novel about this conundrum titled *The Bluest Eye.* She illustrates precisely the effects of self-perceived ugliness on the black family and the ways in which this reality results in relational abuse that, over time, signifies black familial trauma. Among "ugly people," for instance, cursing, physical abuse, and poverty are commonplace. Yet this is more complicated than it appears. The abuse exposes precisely the lack of value many black people find in one another and reprimands them for their unrelenting ugliness. It's as if black people blame each other for being unattractive, as if their looks are some personal failure they could've avoided.

This is what happens to Pecola, the protagonist in *The Bluest Eye*. She is an ugly eleven-year-old black girl or, rather, a black girl who thinks she's ugly. She is raped by her father and consequently pregnant before age twelve. Because of her supposedly despicable unattractiveness, her rape is laid at her own feet. Her mother never confronts her father about the sexual assault, and neighbors wonder what Pecola did to make her father do that to her. She is referred to as "black dirt" into which her father plants his "seed." It's the blackness of the earth that is blamed for the crime—not the father's illegitimate seeding. This twisted thinking, however, is all too common among the self-rejected. Drug abuse is disproportionately high in impoverished black communities precisely because, in my opinion, far too many residents can't find the value of their being. Their ugliness is a foregone conclusion, reinforced by the way people speak to them, treat them, and deny them acts of tenderness. "Bring yo black ass in this house and take yo bath!" or "Don't sit yo nasty black ass on my brand-new furniture!" or "Wash yo black hands before you touch my food!" all teach a child that one's repulsive blackness relegates them to the class of the unwanted. Hence, they don't require excellent treatment because they don't deserve it. They don't demand honor and respect because they've never had it and never believed they should. The assumption of their lives is that they should be happy to be *tolerated*, for being black and ugly is a stain, a fault, a failure one should not expect others to respect.

Some years ago, I read about a study of dark-skinned black children in public schools. It discovered that teachers tend to overlook their raised hands and call upon lighter-skinned black children more often. It also exposed that dark-skinned black children find themselves in detention disproportionate to their light-skinned peers. This isn't surprising. Dark skin, culturally and historically in America, connotes defiance and rebellion—not humility and love of learning. A dark-skinned black child, which is, by this definition, an ugly child, is a problem upon entry. Teachers stand guard against them to protect the sanctity of white kids and exceptional, lighter-skinned black ones. And dark black kids know it. Hence the reason for their rebellion—because they can't figure out why their being is automatically punishable. I would venture to guess that even today, in the American penal system, a disproportionate number of incarcerated black boys are dark-skinned. And not simply dark, but ugly in their own estimation. Dr. Ellis Monk, a Harvard sociology professor, conducted a study in the early 2000s that discovered a correlation between skin color and incarceration. More specifically, data revealed that a dark-skinned black person is 65 percent more likely to be arrested than a white person, whereas a light-skinned black person is only 40 percent more likely. And if this isn't bad enough, dark-skinned black people are 66 percent more likely to go to jail in their lifetimes than a white person, although light-skinned youth are only 36 percent more likely. This is horrific for several reasons: (1) *All* black children are more likely to be imprisoned than *any* white child; (2) dark-skinned black children bear the assumption of criminality. Their complexion, and, by extension, their being is a social liability; and (3) the average American doesn't give a damn. Black youth, especially boys, spend a lifetime glancing over their shoulders, running from trouble when trouble has been sent to destroy them.

Isn't it interesting that, in Hollywood, the same ten black

male and female faces recycle in contemporary movies? Tyler Perry's lead characters, for example, are always drop-dead gorgeous, although not necessarily drop-dead talented. Yet he discovered something: a huge portion of black viewers long simply to see (and perhaps vicariously live through) those few, unquestionably beautiful black bodies on-screen. We're excited to stare at celebrated, exquisite black flesh. Yet, by doing so, black audiences, unknowingly, perpetuate the very aesthetic crisis Tyler Perry pimps—exaltation of the chosen ones. White actors, however, have a different historical reality. Some are good-looking, although many are more talented than beautiful. No one thinks of Anthony Hopkins, for instance, as physically dazzling, although he is unarguably the master of his craft. However, talent is not enough if you're black and in the public eye. We can go back in history and use the likes of Sidney Poitier and Diahann Carroll to make this point. They were both beautiful *and* talented. Yet many of their white contemporaries (Phyllis Diller, Jack Nicholson) were not. And today, the tradition continues. Gabourey Sidibe, an amazing actress of our time, was on none of the lists of black women heartthrobs. Indeed, even after undergoing laparoscopic bariatric surgery, whereby she lost a reported hundred fifty pounds, she is still not seen as a public image of beauty. Her face is too round, her eyes too close together, and whatever other bullshit white and black people think in their twisted Western minds.

This aesthetic crisis manifests in every part of the black world. It is not ironic, for example, that the black LGBTQ community suffers from this same psychosis. A friend in Atlanta asked me, not long ago, "Why do you think gay black men have such a difficult time dating or finding partners when this city overflows with them?" I told him that, from my perspective, most black gay men aren't looking for a partner; they're searching for the sexiest partner. In other words, regular everyday black gay men won't do for them because they don't represent the highest in aesthetic currency among black gay men. Ordinary black gay men are fuckable, but not marriageable; they will do only when the real beauties can't be had. And the real beauties are almost always those masculine-performing gay men who look like Taye Diggs—those whose sexuality is not "clockable" or immediately "detectable."

Funny thing: when I googled "handsome black gay men," all the links took me to porn sites. Then I got it: beauty, among black people, is tantamount to sexual desirability, for the primary use of the black body in America, especially if one is deemed pretty and gay, has been and still is sexual indulgence—to possess it, dominate it, in exchange for its gratification. It cannot be allowed simply to exist. It must be owned, manipulated, and controlled because a beautiful black body is too commodifiable to let it run free. Hence my belief that the NFL, NBA, and other sports agencies pay black men not simply for their athletic prowess, but also for the viewing pleasure of their physicality. This is one arena in which an unattractive black face can still win—if he can present a sculpted black body in its stead. Americans will pay for the allure a black body elicits. That's been true from the inception of this nation. It's still true today. In sports, an ugly black face might be excusable if the body can spark the latent arousal many desire. That alone justifies its existence.

There seems to be a connection between black self-perception and physical health. Various studies have been conducted and written about in health journals, like the one by

E. H. Mereish titled "Discrimination and Depressive Systems among Black American Men: Moderated-Mediation Effects of Ethnicity and Self-Esteem" in which researchers examine the link between black self-esteem and personal health care practices. In July of 1989, the *New York Times* ran an article titled "Doctors See Gap in Blacks' Health Having a Link to Low Self-Esteem." The article reports that poor eating habits and homicide in the black community are disproportionately high partly because of the way people feel about themselves. This is not difficult to imagine. At the cornerstone of the struggle, I contend, is an aesthetic dilemma too complicated for most blacks to reconcile. There is no way to be pretty and thus valuable in a society whose standard of beauty is diametrically opposed to one's features. Consequently, black people spend disproportionate amounts of money, not on healthy food or exercise trainers, but on fake hair and weekly haircuts. The ugly have to *try* to be pretty, at least according to public standards, if someone is to consider them romantically. The fact that the effort is unsustainable turns into greater self-loathing, however, and sometimes results in drug abuse and other forms of violent, self-destructive behavior to cope.

This aesthetic crisis in the black community, the notion that one is irredeemably ugly, is so real as to be marketable for economic gain. In 2009, Chris Rock released a documentary titled *Good Hair*, in which he examines the economic consequences of black self-hatred. Among other things, he explores the financial gain of countries like India whose citizens sell their hair to black Americans. This foreign market makes billions off the black American community each year. The wave cap, frequently worn by black men, suggests that many brothers are happy to get away from the undesirable tight coil of black hair just as weaves relieve many black women of the same. I teach at an HBCU in Atlanta, and on any given day I see young black male heads covered in "do-rags" or see the imprint of the do-rag across their foreheads. Some brothas wear it to bed EVERY night. Some won't sleep without it. When asked why, they often say, "I like my hair wavy—not nappy." What they don't say is what nappy means, what it equals in terms of black aesthetic value. But if one is black, one knows. It's no secret. In fact, it's an achievement to transmute kinky hair into something more silky, more wavy than a knot. This adds to one's quest toward beauty in the black community and in America at large. Even dreadlocks play a role in the maintenance of black self-hatred. Many will disagree, perhaps, but I assert that locks allow black hair to grow *long* and thus be viewed as beautiful by other blacks. Whites have a different response to locks, I believe, but they aren't the focus of this treatise. So suffice it to say that locks give black people aesthetic currency by swinging and moving as we negotiate our way through the labyrinth of self-loathing. How do I know this? Because it's the "in-between stage" of growing locks that black people dread—that point where the hair has begun to lock but isn't long enough to dangle. Countless folks have told me that if they didn't have to endure that stage, they'd have locks. They didn't understand the fullness of their confession. But I did.

One last perpetuator of the black aesthetic dilemma I should mention is contemporary rap videos. I'm horrendously troubled by the ways in which the black body is often shamelessly oversexualized. Now, lest I'm misunderstood, I'm not critiquing rap lyrics here, although some need serious analysis. What I'm interested in are the ways some rap videos situate the sexualized black body as the announcement of black self-worth. This, I think, is a kind of self-rejection, for it implies that the value of being black is its serviceability—not its mere existence. Certainly many will take issue with this position, and, in some ways, that's the point—to ignite conversation around this phenomenon so that black people discover and understand what we're really doing when we put our own bodies back on the auction block. And metaphorically, that's precisely the issue: we're offering our own flesh this time in exchange for applause and public indulgence. We're stripping ourselves naked and inviting the world to see us as "empowered." Yet I'm not sure self-empowerment comes from physical exposure. Rather, I might argue that the most empowered person is the one whose mind is on display and cannot be dismissed. I do understand the freedom of the black body and how years of its exploitation resulted in its shame. And, yes, there is a kind of liberty in its uninhibited presentation. That is undeniable. But the ultimate ecstasy yet unrealized in the black aesthetic is that total freedom of the black body is not in its physical exhibition—that's the auction block syndrome—but in the display of its creative genius. Cardi B's "WAP" and Lil Nas X's "MONTERO (Call Me By Your Name)," for example, are popular visual displays of the black body, but they don't tell me anything new about black beauty. Of course black women are gorgeous. But half their beauty is their internal genius—a fact that seems to escape hip-hop moguls and America in general. Certainly taking ownership of one's sexual freedom and its expression is liberating. No doubt about that. However, to do so under the guise of "Wet Ass Pussy" is to return us, once again, to the auction block where someone else's pleasure of our body is the point. These lyrics do not engender, for me, praise of black women's strength and sexual autonomy. The idea is marvelous, but the execution is self-degrading. Here's how I know: We might cheer for Cardi B or Megan Thee Stallion as they display wet ass pussies on stage, but if this is about the sexual freedom of black women in general, can we also celebrate Sojourner Truth's wet ass pussy? Would you applaud for Grandma's wet ass pussy? Can we imagine Shirley Chisholm and Fannie Lou on stage in those same physical positions? If you winced, then you get my point. The reason this notion is perplexing is because we *honor* these particular women. We revere them. We understand them to be women of high dignity and character. Our ability to dance along as Cardi B and Megan parade wet ass pussy exposes how little character we conceded unto (or expect from) these two sistas. Our lack of critique suggests that any exhibition of a black woman's body, as long as she does it herself, is empowering and uplifting. Well, I don't agree. I simply believe black women's (and men's) bodies are not for public consumption. We've lived that life before. And we hated how it made us feel. Committing the same crime against ourselves does not make it liberating. It exposes, in fact, that often our imagination fails when we begin to construct black agency because, sadly, we conceive freedom in the same terms as our oppressor—just in a different color. Putting our naked bodies on display slaps white folks in the face, we might think, because *they* once owned our bodies, and now we do! Yet the display is not freedom. The display demonstrates one's desire to emulate the actions of those whose power we envy. The secret is to let white folks have their power and their private lusts—without us thinking we need a black version thereof.

The same holds true for men. Lil Nas X's "MONTERO (Call Me By Your Name)" is certainly an explosively creative video and claims space for young black gay men in the hip-hop world, but I don't think it liberates. Not the way it could've. First, the Devil doesn't deserve the pleasure of black male sexuality. The Devil has done nothing to earn the divinity of black intimate space. And being sexual with him is not a compliment. Or an achievement. Why not, instead, ascend into Heaven and make love to a black God? *That* would be liberating! That's who black people truly admire! Take wings from an angel—instead of horns from Satan—and elevate black gay men to the status of the Holy Ones. Kiss God on the mouth, and smile as the world looks on in disbelief. That, my friend, is transformation. That would show that a black gay man can conceive of God as a reflection of his black gay self. *That* would be empowerment.

But, alas.

We have a long way to go before most black Americans see their beauty. Until then, we pay others inordinate amounts of money to "help" us look presentable. This will change only when black people get unafraid to create our own institutions and thus make our own aesthetic rules. We need a black God with nappy hair, y'all, and a black Christ with the same, and black angels and black choir robes in Heaven. We need to stop straightening little black girls' hair then smiling at them with approval. We need to see black children's magic before we alter their appearance. And we need to tell all black children of their glory and splendor. Then, we won't think of our naked, sexualized bodies as our greatest asset. Or fiercest weapon. We'll have new parameters of beauty—someone made the old ones, right?—and grow these notions until every variety of black is celestial. And finally the world will know that, although our bodies elicit untold ecstasy, our minds and spirits beget the real orgasm.

WHEN WE SEE US

Ava DuVernay's masterful retelling of the tragedy of the Central Park Five left me utterly speechless. I sat numb, long after credits had run, and rocked back and forth until my trembling eased. Then, too devastated to cry, I stared through my living room window, wondering what future black people have in this country. Conceiving no answer, I stumbled into the front yard, leaned upon a small tree, and wept. Those were black boys, *my* boys, who'd been left in a penal system that wanted only their absolute destruction. And that's the power of DuVernay's miniseries *When They See Us*—it forces viewers to imagine the real story of the Central Park Five. They were merely kids—Kevin Richardson and Raymond Santana, fourteen; Antron McCray and Yusef Salaam, fifteen; Korey Wise, sixteen—four blacks and one Hispanic who found themselves accused of raping a white woman they'd never seen. They had been romping through New York's Central Park on the afternoon of April 19, 1989. As fate would have it, Trisha Meili, the white woman, was sexually and physically assaulted the same day. The boys were arrested, and, out of sheer fear, lied on each other and named each other as guilty suspects. After hours of grueling coercion, four of them confessed although none of them had done it. No semen found at the crime scene matched any of theirs. Still, they were tried, convicted, and imprisoned for six to thirteen years. Most of them served the majority of their time until the real criminal, Matias Reyes, turned himself in voluntarily. DuVernay holds no punches in illustrating how racist American judiciaries—prosecutors, police, judges, lawyers, and public media—played their parts in the boys' demise. I cried not only for what happened to them, but also because it *keeps happening*, over and over again, and no one seems able or willing to stop it. Even the boys' parents, who obviously love them, didn't know what to do.

All five boys' lives were destroyed. Viewers—and those who followed the real-life events—know that the boys are simply scapegoats for a heinous crime committed against a white woman—isn't it always a white woman?—and therefore someone black must die. It's the oldest cultural trope in America. That's why it works—because, in the American imagination, black boys are the boogeyman from whom all white girls need protecting. It's not hard for most to believe—in fact, it's logical—that several black boys entered Central Park with the expressed desire to rape a white woman. After all, black boys, in the white American psyche, possess some latent criminal gene that predisposes them to such behavior. Their greatest appetite is for white female flesh. This asinine assumption drove prosecutors to run and grab any black boys they could find. It's the same thrust that informed the lynching of countless black men in this country over the years. To be sure, many (if not most) had not even looked at a white woman, much less desired her. Yet their monstrous sexual nature loitered in white people's minds, inviting them to believe that black men stood ready and willing to violate white women at every turn. This is so absurd as to be laughable. But it's the living myth of black male sexual behavior. And it thrives even today. Black fathers, like mine, told black sons, over the years, that white girls are nothing but trouble. "Stay away from them!" they said emphatically. "They'll laugh with you until you touch them, then they'll cry rape, and you'll end up under the jailhouse." Most of us believed them. The ones who didn't often learned the hard way.

(Readers are undoubtedly expecting me to yield that there are good white women and men who are indeed trustworthy and honorable of black flesh, but can we skip this exhausting caveat this time?)

Most incredible about *When They See Us* is not *what* happens but *when*. It's 1989—not 1889. Yet the lies and manipulations, built upon racial attitudes and stereotypes, invite a scenario that resembles the 1950s Emmett Till case or the Scottsboro Boys of the 1930s. I've heard countless millennials say they can't believe such blatantly heinous, intentionally racist acts still occur. Not like that. "Sure, racism exists. But it's not *that* obvious anymore, is it? We thought that chapter was over." Not only is it not over, but one of the main perpetuators of the boys' guilt becomes president of the United States. That's right—Donald Trump destroys the boys' innocence in a New York newspaper ad, for which he paid handsomely, that, in no uncertain terms, condemns the crime and the boys' character. The article is titled "Bring Back the Death Penalty. Bring Back Our Police!" In this missive, he says, "I want to hate these murderers and I always will. I am not going to psychoanalyze or understand them, I am looking to punish them." My contention is that, had this been a few years earlier, Trump might've led an unapologetic march right back to

Central Park where, at dawn, America would've found five black and brown bodies swinging from New York's elm or scarlet oak trees. DuVernay illustrates that belief in the boys' guilt happened almost overnight. Indeed, she forces the contemporary American audience to admit that very little progress has been made on racial issues, especially where the criminal justice system is concerned. She puts in our faces the fact that black boys are not imprisoned because of their criminal nature; rather, they're locked up because of what whites—and some blacks—think they're capable of. The orchestrated dismantling of the Central Park boys in *When They See Us* is so indisputable that many blacks have been left with a serious dilemma: How do we live in America now? We can't hide in naivete anymore. We can't fool ourselves into believing this country wouldn't do to us what it did to our foreparents! We can't act like we don't see this any longer.

In many ways, this has been the blinding effect of pseudo-social progress. And black people have been only too willing to participate. We've softened the truth of racial terror for a contemporary generation whom we hoped wouldn't have to bear the ugliness of America's racial character. We didn't tell our children the full story of our struggle because we wanted them to believe something that wasn't true: the American dream. They needed a dream because our reality was too painful. So we decided to lie, hoping to give black children a clean racial slate from which to function in America. But this move has come to haunt us. We now know that the American dream includes black subjugation. One can't have excess without others having less. We should've taught this so black children understood the social makings of "the haves" and "the have-nots." Survival is easier, I believe, if a person comprehends the nature of their environment and the challenges it poses. This is why today's black and brown parents, like those in *When They See Us*, rail against kids who buck legal authority by asserting presumed agency. Cops kill colored kids who do that. Truth is, we blindfolded these children and sent them into a society that exploits their naivete to justify their demise. Now we seem unable to figure out why so many wander about confused and disillusioned. We've always known there is no real equality in America. We just didn't want to believe it. Because if we accepted this ugly truth, we'd have to explain why we're still here. And most of us think we have nowhere to go.

This means we're stuck. We're trying to pimp a system we know is rigged against us. Most of us simply wonder what few will seep through the cracks. We're not of the illusion that most black people will *ever* prosper. Black (and some white) academics have done the work—see Carol Anderson's *White Rage*, Robin DiAngelo's *White Fragility*, or Isabel Wilkerson's *Caste*—to prove that black subjugation is an intentional, organized social effort. It does not result from laziness or lack of intelligence on the part of black people; it is the fruit of a country that needs black suppression for the continued exaltation of white supremacy. And before white supremacy falls, every black person in America will be destroyed. But again, we know this. Even sympathizing whites who appear to loathe racism can't be found when black life is on the line. They argue against racism and sometimes give money to support causes, but they do not surrender the privileges of white supremacy. They do not volunteer their children's lives in exchange for ours. They do not endow black colleges the way they endow their own. Why should they, you ask? Because black people built theirs, too.

Sufficient research exists to substantiate that black labor erected not just Tuskegee and Tougaloo and Talladega, but also Emory and Brown and Princeton. Everyone in America knows that practically any structure or institution built prior to the 1960s likely includes black sweat. This is how America became great in the first place. Hence, "Make America Great Again" is simply an invitation to another century of oppression—as far as conscious black folks are concerned.

But back to *When They See Us.* DuVernay goes to great lengths to demonstrate how, throughout the Central Park ordeal, white life is valued over black life. The prosecutor, Linda Fairstein, insists that "somebody must pay" for what happened to Trisha Meili. More specifically, she says, "This is an epidemic. We are not in control." Her adamance appears honorable, but its racist undergirding blinds her to the truth. Her anger is fueled not only by the crime itself, but by the notion that some nigga thought he could do this to white flesh and get away with it. The more she considers the crime, the more incensed she becomes until her rage morphs into a crusade to save white feminine virtue. Felicity Huffman plays the part so well that, at times, I forgot she wasn't Fairstein. But Fairstein *is* a white woman who, knowingly or not, is protected via America's hierarchy of beings and thus knows that her word carries weight greater than the black boys' she prosecutes. That's what disturbed me most—knowing that the prosecution had to find someone to charge for this white woman's rape. And someone should be charged! But they weren't interested in finding the rapist; they were committed to making one. So they did. Of course the most believable tapestry from which a rapist in America is made is black male flesh. Step one was to force a confession, and that's precisely what police did. Korey Wise later testified that he was pressured until he broke: "They said if I was there, and if I went along with it, that I could go home. And that's all I wanted. That's all I wanted was to go home. That's all I still want." That these are literally children is often overlooked. They are black and male, and thus already criminalized, so their guilt is an easy assemblage.

Emily Nussbaum wrote an article in the *New Yorker* wherein she declares that the aim of *When They See Us* was, essentially, compassion. "Its main concern," she offers, "its method and its theme is empathy. Not a syrupy, manipulative empathy but a rigorous one, meant as a corrective." For me, this is the voice of quintessential white guilt. The aim of this series is *not* empathy at all. I do not believe Ava DuVernay meant primarily to make America feel sorry for these boys. Rather, I believe she meant to make us mad as hell. I think she meant to spark rage so intense that even if a confrontation broke out in the streets, at least it might move this issue toward public conversation and human action. It's insulting, really, to think that DuVernay's hope was simply to elicit empathy for these boys, since empathy does not translate into social transformation. Not in America. The only thing that initiates change in America is civil disobedience. We've seen this since the days of slave rebellions. Ava DuVernay knows this, and she's bold enough to start shit around the issue of criminal justice reform because, without our anger, nothing will occur.

Actually, DuVernay may be the boldest artist alive right now. *When They See Us* is raw enough, true enough, painful enough, to start a revolution for the salvation of black life in

America. The series was released amid the backdrop and prominence of the Black Lives Matter movement, which has done tremendous work to illustrate the heinous ways in which black bodies are destroyed every day at the hands of an unjust legal system. But it did not stop them from doing it. *When They See Us* presents America's shameful treatment of black people so unapologetically that it should spark consciousness and action, even on the part of the once indifferent. The fury this series engenders is precisely the energy it will take to initiate an overhaul of the American criminal justice system. I pray only that this vehemence spills into the streets until it comes.

When They See Us reminds me of the Dred Scott case. I mentioned it earlier, but let me add that the Supreme Court's ruling had little to do with his argument, for not only did they rule against him, but they declared his humanity nonexistent. They proclaimed that, as a black man, he had no legal right to sue any white man because black people "are not included, and were not intended to be included, under the word 'citizens' in the Constitution, and can therefore claim none of the rights and privileges which that instrument provides for and secures to citizens of the United States." Chief Justice Roger Taney articulated the court's decision, hoping, surely, to establish a precedent and thereby hush abolitionists around the anti-slavery cause. This did not happen. Indeed, things backfired on Taney and resulted, ultimately, in the Civil War. Nonetheless, the point is that both Dred Scott in 1857 and the Central Park Five in 1989 believed they were free and protected by the law. Both assumed themselves citizens of the United States—whether the United States agreed or not—and behaved as if the nation would have their backs.

Of course it did not. Their crime, really, was challenging a system that had already assigned them a zero-sum social designation. They didn't want to be niggas, rapists, property at the whims and social expectation of whites. They wanted to be men and boys, free inhabitants of the country wherein they'd been born and persecuted. The sad thing, of course, is that black people have never enjoyed full citizenship in the United States. We were three-fifths American for a while, then, after ratification of the Fourteenth Amendment, we became Jim and Jane Crow's stepchildren who should be glad simply to exist. Sure, we've been *called* American, and we've even given our lives for this country, but we've never enjoyed the same assumptions as whites. We've never been citizens without an accompanying adjective: colored, Negro, black, Afro, etc.—some special category of Americans who do not share the full privileges of the master class. Those are the *real* Americans, which is why they needn't call themselves "white Americans" unless blacks are around. This would be redundant. Americans, by definition, *are* white.

Ironically, Dred Scott and his family were freed a few months after losing his case. His master decided they deserved manumission and granted it. He owned them, after all, so he had every legal right to determine their social status. And he did. Dred Scott died only a few weeks later, a free man. But to what end? He spent the entirety of his life fighting for a freedom that rested entirely in one white man's hands. Only when that man decided to grant it did Scott breathe the air of freedom. The same happened to the Central Park Five. A white woman prosecutor constructed a racist narrative about a group of young black boys who happened to be in Central Park at the time of the rape, and she convinced a judge and jury of its validity. This didn't take much convincing, since the boys were black, so she secured a guilty verdict quite easily. Most frightening is that Fairstein actually believed the boys raped and mutilated Trisha Meili. She was not trying to falsely frame them; rather, she seemed to have convinced herself that these beautiful black and brown boys were capable of precisely the crime with which they were charged. Never mind that none of the evidence led to them. The myth of black masculinity did the trick. *Only* when a fellow prisoner admitted his own guilt were the boys freed and deemed innocent—after a decade of wrongful imprisonment. And to this day, the woman responsible for the unspeakable tragedy—and Justice Taney for that matter—never admitted wrong or apologized. So far, no legal action has been taken against her.

My point is that black life *still* exists at the whim of white folks. On any given day in America, a policeman can stop a black person, and, within minutes, black life can be extinguished. This is no exaggeration. Ask Philando Castile. Or Eric Garner. Or Michael Brown. Or Dontre Hamilton. Or John Crawford. Or Ezell Ford. Or Tanisha Anderson. Or Tamir Rice. Or Sandra Bland. Or Rumain Brisbon. Or Jerame Reid. Or Tony Robinson. Or Phillip White. Or Eric Harris. Or Walter Scott. Or Freddie Gray. Or Trevon Johnson. Or Eric Logan. Or Jamarion Robinson. Or JaQuavion Slaton. Or Ryan Twyman. Or Brandon Webber. Or Jimmy Atchison. Or D'ettrick Griffin. Or Yvette Smith. Or Miriam Carey. Or Darnesha Harris. Or Malissa Williams. Or Aiyana Stanley-Jones. Are you tired of reading names yet? Well, I'm tired of writing them. And of burying them.

Most absurd is that the City of New York paid the Central

Park Five forty million dollars for their trouble. Of course no amount is honorable, no amount any real compensation for the decade of torture and incarceration these boys endured. Yet somehow the value of black life always gets reduced to dollars and cents. Practically every death mentioned above resulted in some sort of financial settlement—as if America expects black people, once paid, to be satisfied and silent. I suppose this makes sense. We were bought in America—quite literally—and we're still being purchased. Everyone knows that, like on southern plantations, every dollar spent on a black body results in hundreds of thousands of dollars in production. This economic contract—black labor in exchange for white pleasure and privilege—is the original formula of these United States. It's sad that, sometimes, black people play into it, too. Far too often we accept cash as recompense for the exploitation of black life, and, thereafter, do very little to challenge the system that perpetuates it. Perhaps most feel unempowered. Or maybe some feel that money is the greatest—and most useful—reimbursement America can offer.

I beg to differ. While money has its value, especially to typically poor people, it often lulls the mind into a kind of malaise that hinders, if not altogether destroys, social consciousness. Plus, once whites compensate financially, they perceive their responsibility complete. But money won't fix America's racial issues. Apologies won't either. The only thing that will transform our destructively racist society is first admitting that it is destructively racist. We must be mature enough—Baldwin called America *infantile*—to have this difficult conversation that we've avoided since slavery. That's right—we've NEVER had a national conversation about race wherein everyday people participate. We've had plenty of committees on racial reconciliation and race-centered interfaith coalitions commissioned by local, state, and federal bodies, but I daresay that a real exchange, where people get to speak their honest, unfiltered truth about racial terror has been strategically evaded. And I know why. Black and brown people's anger couldn't be restrained. It would get out of control. It would almost certainly result in a brawl because age-old excuses and insincere explanations will only fuel black rage. Police would be on hand, waiting for black people to become unruly and unmanageable, and once again we'd be back where we started. Yet even if it becomes explosive, this conversation needs to occur. Only the willfully naive hope that three centuries of slavery's pain, devastation, and trauma can be purged without volatility. And until that fury is expunged and honored, racial tension will persist in this land of the unfree and home of the unbrave.

The real question posed by *When They See Us* is how do we restore these young black and brown men's mental and psychological health? How do we nurture them into beings whose lives are not shadowed by second glances and condescending pity? Unless and until this happens, we've not honored them. Money does not buy recognition of a person's humanity. It does not correct America's overwhelming readiness to imprison boys of color simply because they're not white. And it certainly does not heal wounds left when, in precious few cases, criminalized boys are proven innocent. We cannot give Kevin and Raymond and Antron and Yusef and Korey new memories in exchange for the horrific ones swirling in their heads. Yet we *can* imprison those public figures who constructed the narrative for their conviction. We *can* advertise these young men's innocence as enthusiastically as we once advertised their guilt. We *can* insist that their story, this documentary, be seen in every school in America. We *can* gather black boys together and touch them and love them and hold them until they know their true value. Then we can take to the streets with our bullhorns and indivisible unity and shout, scream, protest, and fight until, in King's words, the arc of the universe bends toward justice. This we *can* do.

When *WE* see us.

DYING TO BE LOVED

Public health officials wonder why black men are still contracting HIV in disproportionately high numbers. The Centers for Disease Control reported, in 2019, that "black people account for a higher proportion of new HIV diagnoses compared to other races and ethnicities." Black gay men are, by far, the most affected in this group. In fact, more than 9000 black men contracted HIV in 2019, while only 5805 white men and 7820 Hispanic/Latino men discovered their positive status. The real scare is that black men are only 6 percent of the US population. Now, unless we assume black gay men unintelligent, we must believe something is amiss here. I have very close friends in the HIV prevention field who shake their heads whenever we broach this subject. They know, of course, that stigma, unawareness of one's status, and hesitance around PrEP all play a role, but perhaps there's another variable, too, something invisible that many of us haven't considered.

This is painful to write and even more painful to admit, but I think many young black gay men are *willing* to die—if it's the only way to be loved without limits. That's right. They've negotiated with death and they're clear on the terms. One could even say they've *decided* to die in order to be touched fully and freely in this life. Most of them know rejection, debasement, and humiliation, in one way or another, so they don't share the American dream of long life filled with children or some existential joy. They simply want to be loved—completely—like every other human being. They want to *make* love freely, without self-chastisement or guilt. However, the world says their intimacy could kill. Yet, unlike for so many of their queer elders, going "untouched" isn't an option. Gay kids today enjoy full-bloomed boldness that, forty years ago, was only a hope. Hence, some risk lives—their own and others'—as they embrace imperfect, uncondomed bodies, regardless of the cost. Their behavior is certainly liberating. It's also, sometimes, deadly.

Historically, black gay boys have rarely been loved and adored *the way they are*. Many are beaten, by parents and/or homophobes on the streets, with hopes that they'll change, as if their authenticity is somehow personally offensive. Some—far too many—are touched only in reprimand. Parents scold them, preachers pray for them, teachers sneer at them, and they find themselves, at fifteen or twenty, so desperate for love that nothing, including their very lives, is worth not knowing it. Many assume a mask of defiance—that disposition that says "FUCK YOU!" to the world—so their hurt won't completely consume them. Others hide in heteronormativity, performing sufficient masculinity so that others leave them alone. And a few swing to the other extreme—living in bars and sex clubs or surviving through sex work. But all of them do *something*. They construct the best world they can, knowing they won't win, but refusing to die without facing the possibility of love. It's a beautiful thing, really. It just costs so much.

When you're taught that your entire existence is an abomination, you stop hoping for certain things. You learn quickly that love is optional for you. Sex will be dirty and defiled and spoken of only in the crudest terms. You will be prayed for incessantly, but never worshipped. Whispered about, but never exalted. God does not like you, others will say, which justifies their hatred, and makes you wonder what went wrong in the womb that even God couldn't fix. Everything about you is a problem: the way you walk, the way you talk, the shape of your body, the way you hold your hands, the timbre of your voice. Young black gay boys discover very early that, if they are to have value in their community, they'd better come up with some other way of being. Most find something. Many escape into the church, which, of course, is ironic since churches often condemn them, although churches also use them—when they need the spirit to move. And in their young, fragile hearts, this condemnation translates into the belief that they are not lovable—not to the standard majority. So they search for other rejects, like themselves, who *can* love them without concern for their lives.

In the '80s, when AIDS ran rampant in the black gay community, many believed and spoke of the epidemic as God's wrath against sexual deviance. Preachers nationwide shouted unashamedly, "You got to pay for your sins! God is not mocked! A man ain't got no business lying with another man!" They buried sons of the church weekly, warning other boys to "Be men!" the way God intended. Most tried hard. Many even married women, believing, as some had suggested, that *pussy'll change your mind.* Even preachers said this. We heard them. But they were wrong. The only thing marriage did was convince black women that black men were willing to use them, yet again, to hide their disgrace. This was misogyny at its best. It was wrong then. It's still wrong now.

I recall what AIDS did to black men in the '80s and '90s. It drained them of life and happiness. It turned them into community pariahs. It stripped their bodies so angrily that many were left as mere skeletons of their original selves. I had friends who went from 200 pounds to 135 pounds in a matter of weeks. They looked unplugged from life's source: shriveled, withdrawn, bedridden. Relatives hid them away in dark rear rooms and unashamedly lied about their malady. "Cancer," some said, shaking pitiful heads. Or "Doctors don't know what it is." We weren't told to love them; we were told to shun them. "God hates the sin, but loves the sinner" turned into "God hates the sinner, too." So many died of AIDS during that era that some black gay men simply stopped having sex altogether. They became eunuchs of fear. They'd been made to despise their own desires, to believe that their natural urges were demonic, so they simply stepped into abstinence. This, however, did not make others love them. It simply meant they wouldn't die from *the thing.* That's how people thought of AIDS—as some monstrous epidemic that sought to find and admonish black men for their sissyhood, their sexual recalcitrance. We now know better. But then, many black women married masculine-performing gay men and paid for it. In other words, ignorance around homosexuality cost lives in the entire black community. It still does.

Young people today are not quite so fearful. They seem to have less to lose. American culture is more tolerant, more supportive, more nurturing of variant identities than forty years ago, so current LGBTQ millennials take risks once unheard of. This is not to say that being gay is somehow easier than it once was; rather, it's to assert that the contemporary LGBTQ community has far more allies than its predecessor ever did, and therefore black gay boys can consider modes of being that their elders never conceived of. The decision to love without limits, literally to forego all barriers to the pleasure of the HIV-positive body, is both a declaration of agency and a choice—albeit, perhaps, unwise—not to treat oneself as too diseased to love.

If you're over forty, you remember the emaciated ones, those whom AIDS swallowed whole. You remember the oxygen tanks and white face masks. You couldn't forget the way families sometimes abandoned brothers in stale, dank hospital rooms. You recall that many fathers and mothers wouldn't endure open-casket funerals. They didn't want the shame. We shook our heads. We knew. They knew we knew. But we weren't free to talk about it, to mourn the loss of our sacred brothers. No. Their untimely demise was supposed to function as a warning to the rest of us that Death was on its way to every household where boys refused to be boys. So, hypermasculinity became every boy's burning desire. It wasn't always accessible though. Or believable. Many gay boys were simply too effeminate. But they tried. Some died trying.

The legacy of this epidemic was that black gay boys were taught the ugliness of their desires. They were made to believe that God hates their intimacy. This is a horrible inheritance for any human being—the realization that their affection kills. But this is what happened. This became the narrative for black gay men of the '80s. Since, back then, no one knew who had HIV until it was too late, a large portion of black men, unlike their more empowered descendants, simply denied themselves the right to love. Or at least to express it.

The larger public, it seemed, was delighted that faggots were finally getting their due. Even medical officials were slow to respond to this public health crisis. After all, only sissies were dying. And black sissies at that. White gay men, who certainly experienced discrimination and abuse, were at least socially valued for their whiteness. Yet no one could imagine why a black boy would want to be that way, when simply being black was already hard enough. Some still believe, even today, that people choose to be gay. Yet, for the life of me, I can't conceive why anyone would.

Still, the only way to survive, it seemed then, was through avoidance. Many black gay brothers simply resolved to live out their days alone. Often, mothers kept them close and loved them privately, but even they, many of them, couldn't love them openly. Friends and relatives learned not to ask about their private lives or love interests. If they were alive, people thought, they had avoided the others. There were, of course, bold, stalwart black men like Essex Hemphill and Marlon Riggs who defied the imprisonment of silence, who told the world to kiss their ass if it thought they were going to die in shame. And we loved those men. We exalted them. But most of us were not like them. We were afraid to die in shame, afraid of shaming our people to death. So we lived—some of us—but now we wonder if dying in our truth might've been better. Our silence did not protect us from public ridicule. It did not make America rethink her toxic homophobia. It did not heal our hearts from fear of death. It did not make hateful people love us. It did not engender dignity or understanding in the heart of the ignorant. Ultimately, it did not save us. No, our silence only prolonged the inevitable confrontation between our potentially free, living selves and the pseudo-freedom we had constructed. We didn't know then what Essex and Marlon knew—that a man will either live free or regret that he didn't.

And that's the point here—that contemporary black gay men won't accept silence anymore. They won't agree to shut up and jack off alone until their dying day. They're insistent about their humanity, resistant to the notion that there is no Heaven for them, even if they enter earlier than most. They have help in places black gay men of the '80s only dreamed of. There are books now—Saeed Jones's *How We Fight for Our Lives*, Hari Ziyad's *Black Boy Out of Time*, George M. Johnson's *All Boys Aren't Blue*, my own *Perfect Peace*, etc., etc.—and movies like *Moonlight* and *B-Boy Blues* and even churches like Atlanta's Vision Cathedral, pastored by a visionary black gay man (and his husband) who celebrate sexual variance in the kingdom of God. None of this was available forty years ago. And if black men today must die to live their truth and to love without fear, that is precisely what many are prepared to do.

They don't say this. They don't even admit it. It's often a subconscious conviction, a kind of inadvertent decision not to err as their fathers did. They simply refuse the condom. Or reject the meds. Or avoid asking the lover's status. But they know. These are intelligent black men who've had to negotiate worth and communal value most of their lives. They know. It's just not the central question: "Are you positive?" The central question is "Can you love me if I am?" And those who say yes risk it all, knowing full well what that *all* might mean.

Consequently, PrEP hasn't caught on within the black community the way medical officials hoped it would. First, people simply don't die from AIDS the way they once did. The taboo hasn't vanished—that's for sure—but medical advances assure that HIV-positive men don't bear the look of death anymore. Indeed, if a brother takes his meds faithfully, his life expectancy equals that of any other person. So men are not nearly as afraid as they once were. That's one reason being HIV positive and/or spreading the virus is no longer an obsession. Yes, it still kills, but so what? "Black men are dying in the streets anyway," one young brother told me. "So all we want is to love and be loved," he said. "What else really matters?"

Another young man, sitting in my office weeping silently, asked one day, "Where are the old, happy, black gay men?" Our eyes met, but I didn't speak. I couldn't. I had no answer. I could've said, "Here they are!" but I wasn't the age he meant. He was asking for the senior elders, the seventy-five-, eighty-year-olds who had survived AIDS and lived to tell about it. I wanted to assure him they exist, but I didn't know of any. Then I realized the problem: this young brutha couldn't see himself in the future. Neither could I. But I began to wonder... What *does* happen to black gay men as they age? They don't *all* die young, do they? Surely that's not even possible. Wouldn't that be a national disaster?

For his seminal text *Sweet Tea* (2008), scholar E. Patrick Johnson interviewed an old black gay man from New Orleans named George Eagerson or Countess Vivian. At the time, he was grand, flashy, spunky, and ninety-six years old. I'd never heard of this before—a proud black gay man who was practically ancestral. He died in 2012 at age ninety-nine. *But where are the others?* I thought. He can't be the only old black gay man. Yet perhaps he *could be* the oldest *out* black gay man. As I read the interview, Mr. Eagerson morphed into an anomaly in my mind, a sort of cultural dinosaur who had somehow endured. I wanted him or someone to tell me where all the black gay elders had gone.

Countess had no answers. He testified that young black gay men were plentiful in his day. He said, "There were lots and lots of black gays. They were all over the place!" I frowned. "They're all dead now, of course," he said, which makes sense at ninety-six, yet the answer I seek to ferret out is where do gay men go after sixty? If there are hundreds of thousands of young black gay boys, there should be communities of senior black gay men somewhere. But where?

I asked a friend about this and he said something most remarkable: "They discover the futility of homosexuality and leave that lifestyle altogether. Being fabulous and rebellious is cute at twenty-five, but when a man wakes up at forty-five with no one beside him and no one to call, he accepts what people have been telling him all his life—*there is no future in that way of being.*" I almost cried. Not because of the hopelessness, but because of a world that is happy to see these human beings go away. It's as if people think being gay is a fantasy that, at some point, fizzles out. I tried to refute his argument—"black gay men don't simply transmute into heterosexuality over night!"—but I couldn't withstand his recurring question: "Then where are they?"

I discovered, finally, the core of his quandary: he didn't know the utility of LGBTQ folks in a community. He hadn't seen them central to groups of people who *were not* gay. He didn't know why the world needed them. Most of the world doesn't either. But I do. There is no whole, healthy community without gay and lesbian brothers and sisters. Truth is, all beings are necessary in a social system. In the groundbreaking book *The Spirit of Intimacy*, Sobonfu Somé explains that, among the Dagara people of traditional West Africa, those with variant sexualities are seen as particularly spiritual. Their sexuality is understood as a sign of their ability to commune with both the visible and the invisible. They are known as *gatekeepers*, she says, because, metaphorically, they stand at the crossroads between the living and the ancestral realms. "We needed them," she admits, "to negotiate for the rest of us concerning things we cannot know or handle."

We also need queer beings because procreation isn't always bodily. Sometimes it's intangible, resulting in things like the end of oppression and the formation of healing institutions. But rest assured there is no communal vitality without the fluidity of difference. Gay brothers and sisters reveal to the world the many manifestations of love, the multiple ways human beings demonstrate God's divinity. LGBTQ spirits assure that answers and solutions to social dilemmas represent the complexity of who we are and what benefits the greatest whole. And queer people exist to divulge the full human capacity for creative genius. There is no artistic tradition without us. No Broadway, no American Music Awards, no Pulitzer Prizes, no MacArthur Geniuses, no Harlem Renaissance, no Black Arts Movement, no Woodstock, and certainly no Coachella. Put simply, American culture would not exist without gay people's influence. Actually, culture can only be maintained by those tough enough, bold enough, and imaginative enough to disrupt what ordinary folks find acceptable. When we recognize this, we'll also find those old black gay elders, lurking perhaps in an unsatisfying heteronormativity, and we'll free them to be what God sent them to be. Until then, many black gay boys today agree to die because, after the rendezvous of youth, their imaginations fail to reveal any reason to press forward into an unknown tomorrow. We—black folks, America, the Western World—will answer one day for having dismissed the beauty of these sacred souls, and on that day, I hope the whole world is listening when God whispers, very softly, "I'm gay, too."

THE BEAUTY AND STRUGGLES OF HBCUs

The 2017 movie *Hidden Figures* exposed to the world what black college graduates already know—that HBCUs graduate some of the most brilliant people on the planet. I sat in the theater smiling as the story of Katherine Johnson unfolded. Finally, the truth of black schools was being revealed. I wasn't so much awed by Johnson's abilities—black schools have been producing extraordinary scholars since their inception—but rather by the teachers she must've had. And not just her, but all the black women, the "computers," working in the basement at NASA in the '60s, doing complicated mathematics by hand. And all of them, no doubt, proud alumni of historically black schools.

As a graduate of and current professor at Clark Atlanta University, I know firsthand the miracle of black college teaching. So does Jelani Favors, whose *Shelter in a Time of Storm* chronicles the tremendous tradition of activism and academic excellence within the nation's HBCUs. Even with their foibles and financial woes, these schools have resurrected the dead in many instances and made brick without straw. They have assumed the intelligence of black youth when America deemed them uneducable. They have invested in a collective black future that no one else cared to dream. Black college professors and administrators are clear that, each August, we inherit the rejected, the maltreated, the brilliant though self-doubting, and, often, the self-loathing. We accept them nonetheless, even, sometimes, against the justification of high school transcripts and marginal SAT/ACT scores. Everyone knows the deal concerning black kids and public education. Black colleges do everything possible to reverse this effect. Faculty know that sagging pants does NOT denote stupidity. Or that a long, flowing weave does not automatically announce self-hatred. Or that smoking weed does not equate to a poor GPA. These are modern stereotypes of black youth. We get this. And because of this, we welcome kids—beautiful, brilliant, magnificent kids—who otherwise might never know the transformative power of higher education. However, this often means that black schools sign an impossible contract. We promise to do what the world cannot imagine—plant, weed, and harvest a quality college education in (sometimes) poorly prepared black kids. This is a gargantuan task, to be sure. Yet black colleges know that a struggling academic record is not indicative of one's academic abilities.

The real work, however, is convincing black kids of their own intellectual prowess. Many believe what teachers and parents have told them—that they are unintelligent, trade school material, and, ultimately, unnecessary. I know this because countless students over the years have objected when I celebrated their superior minds. They've said things like, "You just tryin' to blow up my head, Dr. Black!" or "Please don't play with me. That's not funny." Or "I ain't never made good grades." When I've asked, "What does that have to do with your true genius?" many respond, with a look of surprise:

"How else would you know if I'm smart?" They've believed, their whole lives, that their grades and test scores announce their intellectual parameters. I believed that once, too—until discovering ways in which systemic racism works to maintain a permanent underclass of blacks in America whose lives depend upon their menial service. This has been true since the arrival of Africans in this country. We have, most of us, always been relegated to hard, poorly paid physical labor. We've chopped cotton, harvested tobacco, broken mules, built houses, repaired fences, birthed babies (ours and others'), cleaned homes, chauffeured lazy-ass landowners, dug ditches, laid railroads, built highways, led wars, cleared land, built cars, fixed hair, stacked bricks, caught and butchered wild game, trapped furs, then entertained white folks *after* these tasks were completed. Some of us were entrepreneurs and writers, too, but very few. Most black people, then and now, earned their living through very physical means. It's what we as a country are used to seeing black people do. It's what we *want* black people to do. "Get you a trade and you'll never be hungry," elders once told me. "College don't guarantee no job!" Bless their hearts. They, like so many others, didn't know that true education isn't about a job anyway.

Black kids, often hoping against hope, fill the halls of HBCUs every fall, wondering how the educational process will be different this time. What they find is something far more difficult than what they've known. This is because the expectation of their intelligence is now nonnegotiable. Heretofore, it was always unfixed, always flexible, always dependent upon variables beyond their control. Yet, now, because their worth is assumed, they are often frustrated by poor grades and standards that seem too rigid. Truth is, they are simply encountering, many for the first time, the *assumption* of their intelligence. This is life altering. Many—I daresay most—have embraced mediocre personal standards because few authority figures ever demanded more. Because of this, grades at HBCUs can be comparatively lower than grades at PWIs (Predominantly White Institutions). This reflects only the fact that HBCU students are expected to perform as well as students anywhere—although they've often not been *prepared* to do so. The resulting tension frustrates students and professors alike, but the standard is correct. We know this for sure. Students who endure this hard love usually end up distinguishing themselves as first-rate in their disciplines. Countless examples prove this. Indeed, prior to the '80s, extraordinary African Americans in practically every field boasted HBCU matriculation. To say these institutions work miracles is neither an exaggeration nor an overstatement. It is simply the truth. And we'll continue doing so—as long as people continue assuming the inferiority of black children.

I am a product of an HBCU that did for me what no PWI could've done. I entered Clark College in the fall of 1984, and immediately encountered genius I'd never seen in black. Professors assigned papers and gave exams that challenged me beyond my wildest imagination. I recall an essay exam, in Freshman Comp, which required us to write three essays in an hour. I had never written so much in so little time. When I got the exam back and saw the 95, I danced (literally) as my self-worth bloomed. I had gone to school with white kids in rural Arkansas—smart white kids who had been very kind to me—but I had not experienced black scholarly excellence. Not yet. Then, at Clark College, as part of the honors program, every student, every teacher was smart beyond measure. I suppose I was smart too, but they seemed smarter than me. The books we read were black authored; the history we studied was black centered; the lectures we heard were black voiced. My identity took shape; I learned what it meant to be an African in the world. New names were planted in my consciousness: Wole Soyinka, Toni Morrison, Imhotep, Fannie Lou Hamer, James Baldwin, Ann Petry, Julian Bond, Stokely Carmichael. I loved these people, my people, their stories, their unthinkable achievements, and I began to love myself. They looked like me. They knew what I knew. They had survived what had been designed to kill them. So had I. So maybe, like them, I too had something to say to the world.

First semester sophomore year, I took a class that changed my life forever. It was titled History of the English Language. There was nothing extraordinary to me about the subject itself, but the professor was the most noted linguist in the Southeast. I didn't know this then. I simply entered the classroom and sat down, hoping to do well. I'd heard from other students about Dr. Leroy Martin, how he challenged students and never gave As. But I needed one. I was on full scholarship and couldn't afford a B. So, determined to disrupt his reputation, I sat in the front row, prepared to give my all. By far, it was the hardest course I've ever taken—PhD classes included—but definitely the most rewarding.

On day one, Dr. Martin entered with no books, no notes, no nothing. Only an unbroken piece of chalk. He warned, without introduction, that he was not to be played with. "There are no makeup exams, no late papers, no excused absences," he announced boldly. "None. Of any kind. For any reason." We shivered in silence. There were seven students in the class—six girls. I, the only boy, knew this would be an uphill battle. Dr. Martin had heard of me, he said, of my "stellar academic performance," and seemed determined to bring me down to size. "I understand, Mr. Black, that you are quite distinguished in our department. Is that correct?"

I was embarrassed, but I had to answer. "Yessir," I murmured.

He nodded. "Very good. What is your GPA?"

I glanced at my colleagues, all of whom hung their heads. "I have a four point O, sir."

His eyes bulged, then he offered coolly, "You do NOT! You have a four point *zero*, young man. O is a letter."

I have never forgotten that distinction, nor have I forgotten the importance of sharp details and high standards, which, ultimately, was his point. He proceeded to speak of phonemes, morphemes, lexemes, diphthongs, fricatives, bilabials, and other lexicon I had never heard of. It seemed his intention to intimidate me, and he succeeded. But I had no choice. It was required of all English majors, as a prerequisite for some upper-level courses, and only he taught it. He boasted that only he *could* teach it. Most girls in the class were juniors who had already failed it once or twice. I was the only sophomore. Still, that didn't matter to him or the institution. I had to take the class, so I did.

We had hours of homework every night. Dr. Martin walked us through the development of the English language, from grunts and utterances in ancient caves to the present era. He didn't care that we possessed no prerequisite knowledge; that was our problem. "Read whatever you must," he said, "in order to understand this subject completely." And I meant to understand, so I read unassigned books and articles unto exhaustion. On the first exam, Dr. Martin gave me—and I do mean *gave me*—an 89.5. I was furious. "What the hell is an 89.5?" I complained to the department chair, who warned me to be cool. Dr. Martin didn't take well to student criticism. I had done fine, she said. Far better than any other student, she was sure. And she was right. The next highest score was a 65, Dr. Martin announced proudly, so I let it go. But I worked even harder, convinced that an A was still within reach.

One of the course requirements was a research paper. Dr. Martin announced midsemester that he would disseminate topics during the next class period. I raised my hand, confused, and asked what he meant. After staring at me for several belittling seconds, he said, "I have sculpted research topics specifically for each of you, according to your capacity and abilities." Then he stared some more. I looked away. Only then did he add, "I have no confidence *whatsoever* that any of you could conceive an idea whereby I'd be even the *least bit* enlightened." I covered my mouth in horror. *Is this man serious? What an ass.* But sure enough, when he entered the next class session, he bore large manila envelopes with our names written on the front in his gorgeous, calligraphic penmanship. He called us up, and we marched like sinners approaching the Judgment Seat. We were instructed not to open envelopes until all had been distributed. When I opened mine, tears streamed: "You are to examine the development of modern prefixes and suffixes in rural Appalachian spoken dialect." *What?* How in the world was I to do this? I had never heard an Appalachian dialect. When I inquired, Dr. Martin said, "I suggest you find recordings of such voices or, perhaps, go to the Appalachian Mountains yourself." What? How the fuck was I supposed to do that? His stern gaze signaled that he was dead serious—and that there would be no further discussion. I left the classroom boiling with rage. Others got topics far more accessible, far easier to research. They felt sorry for me, they said. I shouldn't have been so smart.

I didn't know what to do, but I knew one thing for sure: Leroy Martin had another thing coming if he thought I was going to take an F on the assignment. Or even a C. I went to the library and found a few recordings of Appalachian songs, which didn't help very much. A library assistant told me of a novel by Thomas Wolfe—*Look Homeward, Angel*—that might give me a sense of the regional dialect, and although I enjoyed the book, its setting wasn't sufficiently contemporary to meet the requirements of the paper. I thought to return to Dr. Martin for assistance, but he'd made it clear he had nothing more to say. I became anxious; I began to panic. Friends comforted me and told me not to let the assignment destroy me. I didn't intend to do that, but I also didn't intend to ruin my GPA.

With no other choice, I gassed up my car and headed toward the Appalachian Mountains. That's right—I drove there alone, cursing Dr. Martin every mile. This was the fall of 1985. I stopped at general stores and gas stations where I heard local vernaculars and expressions to use in my paper. Folks were surprisingly kind. They were poor, visibly so, but they spoke loudly with spunk that reminded me of white folks in Arkansas, where I was from. I saw only a few black people and they warned me to be careful, which I took to mean get out before dark. That had already been my plan. Yet as I listened throughout the day, I heard raspy, singsong expressions that poured from rural mountain people like rain. It was beautiful, their speech, filled with music and tinges of pain. My tape recorder did its job, and by dusk, I was back on 75 south, headed to Atlanta. I'd found enough secondary sources to support my paper; now I had primary material to defend an argument I'd never before conceived.

When, weeks later, Dr. Martin returned papers, I trembled, refusing to look at the grade. Classmates urged me to be strong, to confront it head-on. But I couldn't look while in front of him. So immediately after class, we gathered outside, and I eased the paper from another large manila envelope. Turning each page as if it were the Word of God, I noticed no markings anywhere. Nothing. No grammatical corrections, no rephrasing of sentences, no objections to any of my assertions. It was as if he'd never read it, which I knew wasn't true. Friends frowned and showed their papers, bleeding with markings and comments galore—Dr. Martin always graded in red—and I became increasingly confused. "What grade did you get?" they asked, but I was too afraid to know. Then, I took a deep breath and turned to the final page with my eyes shut tight. My friends gawked in silence. There, resting at the bottom of the page, was a beautifully drawn and circled B++. No explanation, no critique, no praise. Nothing.

"What kinda shit is that?" one girl screeched finally.

"This man needs his ass whipped!" another said.

"It's better than any grade any of us got."

All of them had received Ds or Fs. Still, I wasn't pleased. If the paper needed no corrections, then in my mind it should've received an A. My ego wouldn't let me drop the matter. Within minutes I knocked on Dr. Martin's office door, and when he said, "Come in, Daniel," I went boldly. Afterward, I realized he'd been waiting for me.

"Dr. Martin, forgive me," I began respectfully, "but I don't understand this grade."

He smiled, something he rarely did, and said, "Mr. Black,

you have done what few students *ever*—" he shouted the word "—do. You have impressed me."

He paused as if something profound had been said, as if I should've been satisfied with this truth. I was not.

"Apparently not very much," I offered, "because I didn't earn an A, although I think I should've. You didn't mark anything wrong, sir!"

"And there is nothing wrong with the paper, Mr. Black. Not *essentially*."

"Essentially? I don't understand."

"It's the best paper I've received in years." His eyes bulged; mine narrowed.

"Then why the B++?"

Dr. Martin stood. "Because it is not the absolute best paper *you* could have written."

"Sir?" I screeched, confused.

"There's nothing wrong with the paper, Daniel, but it's not your *absolute* best. You have another level of brilliance in you."

I left. Outside his door, I collapsed against the wall and cried. I couldn't hold it anymore. I wasn't angry with him; I was disappointed in myself. I knew places in the paper that weren't as polished as I had hoped, and *that* was his point. It wasn't *my* A. I revered Dr. Martin's intellectual opinion, and, this time, he deferred to me. He forced me to critique *myself*, to assess the value of what I had done *on my own terms*, and I understood. He'd taught me not to wait for another person's assessment, even his own, before I knew the value of my own work. It's a lesson I've never forgotten.

These were the kinds of transformative experiences I had at Clark College. Various professors—Dr. Jocelyn Jackson, Dr. Janice Liddell, Dr. Gloria Blackwell, Dr. Ernestine Pickens—

had such high expectations for me that I *wanted* to achieve simply to make them proud. I'd come from poor black people in rural Arkansas who'd taught the value of an elder's asé, so I worked hard to get it.

I recall submitting a paper to Dr. Liddell for African American Lit II. In it, I'd analyzed the symbol of the rat in Richard Wright's *Native Son*. Her comments at the end of the paper read, "Extraordinary. So much was not required." I smiled and pestered her for extra readings until I graduated. She introduced me to Caribbean literature, and I couldn't get enough. I went to her house on weekends and read and borrowed books until I had amassed enough knowledge to boast a minor in Caribbean studies, although I'd never had a formal class. Still, I could discuss the works of Edgar Mittelholzer, Camara Laye, Earl Lovelace, Erna Brodber, Derek Walcott, Paule Marshall—*The Chosen Place, the Timeless People* is still one of my all-time favorites—Jamaica Kincaid, Michelle Cliff, and E. R. Braithwaite because Dr. Liddell gave me these books and made time for me to discuss them with her in her office and home. We became so close that I babysat and mentored her youngest son. This was the magic of a black college experience.

I was learning about *myself*, *my* people, the general grandeur of blackness, and I couldn't get enough. In Dr. Jocelyn Jackson's Honors English course, we read a book titled *Things Fall Apart*. I had never read African authors before, but something about this book felt strangely familiar. I didn't know then that I was African. I knew my ancestors had *come from* Africa, but I didn't claim the continent as home, as a place of personal identity. As we studied Achebe's masterwork, it dawned on me just how African I was. The rituals, the father-son conflict, the proverbs all reminded me of home. Okonkwo was my father in every way. He was patriarchal, harsh, hardworking, and despising of effeminate boys. We had turbulent years because of this. Yet by reading the book, I understood my father differently. He also mirrored Okonkwo in that he loved his people, his traditions, his God. He believed part of his responsibility was to raise sons to be strong, self-assured, and indestructible. He did that. Yet both men's downfall was their inability to adjust, to learn something new, to hear the admonition of a child and grow from it. I shook my head when I finished that book. I knew, finally, which parts of my father I could celebrate and which parts I could live without. I'd soon learn the same for HBCUs.

The central problem with most HBCUs is their desire to emulate PWIs. In other words, HBCUs often seek to mimic majority institutions in terms of what they teach and why. In fact, the mission statements are often pretty identical: "to prepare students to thrive in a global economy." Or some such vague, "universal" wording. This appears laudable, but truthfully, it's misguided. The ultimate function of HBCUs—the paradigmatic structure that *should* govern these sacred places—is to teach the history, achievements, and cultural evolution of African people from antiquity to the present. This would make HBCUs particular and peculiar in ways that would justify their continuous existence. As is, HBCUs are too similar to mainstream institutions for their exorbitant tuitions to make sense. They should not be preparing students to work for white enterprises or to be accepted as graduate students into Ivy League bastions of egotism. Rather, if HBCUs taught self-knowledge as the basis of their entire curriculum, black students would evolve into innovative, creative graduates even more superior than many of the institutions' accomplished alumni. I believe this firmly. Having earned a PhD in African American Studies, I remember, quite endearingly, the transformation of my spirit as I learned who I was, where I'd come from, and the dimensions of my potential. Some of this knowledge began at Clark College, but not enough of it. There are no words to describe the feeling I experienced in graduate school at Temple University when I discovered the breadth and depth of African brilliance and survival. That, dear reader, is true education: the acquisition of knowledge that reinforces a person's worth and value in the world. Presently, very few, if any, black colleges require black history of all its graduates. I do not mean some freshman course that appears to center upon the role of a few black people in world history. I mean extended inquiry into the intellectual history of African people and how they've shaped the world everywhere they've gone. This is a tall order, I know, but such focus would change the relevance—and retention rate—of HBCUs today.

One might assume that attending a black college assures students a black-centered education, but this is not necessarily true. Indeed, HBCUs were not founded for the purpose of teaching black youth self-knowledge; they were founded in order to prepare newly freed slaves for paid servitude. Since their inception, HBCUs have prided themselves on putting black graduates in "positions" of employment that increase the efficacy of black respectability. This has certainly been a worthwhile endeavor, for, without it, there would be no black middle class, and few would argue against the impact of educated blacks on black social upward mobility. Yet now, in an age when black kids can attend almost any school they choose, only a unique, specialized curriculum justifies tuition three times that of most state schools. And it only makes sense that the curriculum should be African centered, because this knowledge—this awareness of the trials and triumphs of black people everywhere—is the only knowledge that will change black students and free them to discover that the point of education is not to get a job. It's the ability to create jobs and to know God as the self regardless of the job. We need innovation—not regurgitation. But you don't teach innovation. You teach self-worth, then innovation follows. For, in truth, innovation is simply one's willingness to risk one's own ideas. That requires the belief that one's intelligence is sufficient to inspire others to invest in it. Only self-love begets this. Only self-love will free black kids to create their own paradigms of success that do not mirror (and do not need to mirror) anything they've already seen.

One doesn't need to come to an HBCU to study Shakespeare or marketing or Freud, although one certainly can. These subjects are accessed for a far cheaper price and with similar excellence at practically any PWI. This is one reason white students graduate in greater numbers than black college students. These subjects, put simply, teach the supremacy of whiteness. White students see themselves *as* Shakespeare and *as* Pavlov, *as* Kierkegaard and *as* Abraham Lincoln, the same way black students see themselves *as* Steph Curry and LeBron James, *as* Nicki Minaj and Kendrick Lamar and Beyoncé. They don't wonder *if* they can be these folks; they wonder when their turn will come. But don't miss the point. Black students are not born knowing or loving sports and entertainment; rather, they see these careers as viable because the culture presents them in black terms and thus they believe they are inheritors of the craft. Until we treat education likewise, disproportionate numbers of black youth will continue to struggle intellectually and trust most the commodification of their bodies for their secure employment. It's what they've seen, what they've been taught, as trustworthy since our genesis in this country.

How much sense does it make, for example, that a music major at an HBCU is not required to study gospel music? To know the talent and stage presence of, say, James Cleveland and Clara Ward? This is systematic self-hatred at its best. Truth is, a music curriculum at an HBCU should be composed of courses such as The African Drum 215, The Field Holler and Ring Shout 312, The Birth of the Blues 350, Great Jazz Artists 412, Seminar in John Coltrane 455, James Cleveland and the Gospel Choir Movement 310, and so on until one is steeped in the knowledge of how black music has influenced the world. That would make HBCU music majors priceless. Yet the problem is that HBCU officials—black people, no less—can't imagine how such knowledge alone constitutes a quality education. Since their inception, HBCUs have been preoccupied with garnering the praise and affirmation of white folks—those who have the money to legitimize their efforts. Said differently, these institutions obsess over validation from external sources, which, ironically, cheapens their originality.

At one point, I thought the accreditation authorities were the problem. Then I learned that they don't determine what schools teach; they make sure schools have the means—professors, library resources, etc.—to teach what they propose and that they have effective instruments of assessment to determine how well (or poorly) they do it. This means, then, that HBCUs teach what they believe will make students most successful in life. Again, the failing, I believe, is that this includes too much deference to Western notions of success and knowledge.

I've spoken about this to colleagues at HBCUs over the years, and all too often was told "The world isn't just black, Dr. Black. It's diverse, and we're preparing our students for success in a global market." But a black student's world *is* black. And that's where we should begin our education of them. Also, interestingly enough, we appear to exclude Africa in our perception of this "global market." How do I know this? Because at most HBCUs, the foreign languages offered suggest that black youth need to prepare to speak to European or Asian nations—not African ones. Few perceive the need for black children to speak Swahili or Twi or Yoruba because few believe Africans matter in the larger global economy. Yet even if African nations are not as internationally influential as, say, Russia or China, black students should be encouraged to learn African languages because these are the tongues of their ancestors. This is a question of identity, of self-worth, of self-preservation. It's important that children are not estranged from their mother tongue. Indeed, when children speak the language of their people, they also access parts of their cultural and spiritual traditions normally inaccessible to them. They come to understand themselves and their inheritance in historically significant ways and begin to believe that they are part of an antiquity far greater than their present moment. This is critical for black American children because they've been taught that their history begins with slavery. Much of the truth and beauty of who they are, who their people were, is bound in the tongues of their ancestors. Learning this tongue, then, unlocks a facet of black uniqueness that no other knowledge can afford. Yet most schools require French or Spanish or Chinese, suggesting that black children should prepare to engage everyone on the world stage *except* indigenous African people.

I've taught at Clark Atlanta University for thirty years now. I clearly believe in HBCUs and know all too well the price of sustaining them. I've met black kids so brilliant, so gifted, so talented I've cried beholding them. Many have become sons and daughters of mine for life. That's what we do at HBCUs—we fill gaps in black cultural and social development so that our students are both educated and made whole. This means we—committed faculty, staff, and administrators—feed students daily, purchase books to help them pass courses, hug and hold them in the midst of life's tragedies, linger on campus well past office hours for emotional and spiritual support, and, most significantly, accept a fraction—and I mean a *fraction*—of our colleagues' pay in order that black children do not, once again, get shafted by a system that can never find adequate resources to support them. It is impossible to enumerate the sacrifices of HBCU personnel, but suffice it to say that we, the truly committed (and this is NOT everyone), have exchanged our lives for the hope of black success. It is an expensive hope.

But isn't hope always?

NOWHERE TO HIDE (OR THE DREAM OF THE CLOSET)

Much as I desired, I never had a closet. Far too effeminate from the start, I couldn't hide my sexuality although Lord knows I tried. As early as first grade, adults called me *sissy*. Kids said *faggot*—harsher word, but same meaning. Scholars said *queer*—stranger word, but same meaning. Church mothers said *sweet*—softer word, but same meaning. Older boys said *punk*—ugly word, but same meaning. Deacons said *funny*—awkward word, but same meaning. All these words meant to describe me, and I knew what none of them meant. *Funny* was particularly troublesome since nothing was funny about me. People's chuckles when they beheld me were derisive and cynical. Sometimes they even asked my parents, "Think he'll ever outgrow it?" My folks shrugged. I'd wanted their anger, their protest, their belligerence as a sign that they didn't agree with others' opinion of me. But they did. Their silence confirmed it. So, they couldn't help me. They didn't even try.

At age five, I began playing the piano and thus lost all possibility of a closet. Now people knew for sure what I was. Not only did I play, but I sang and danced, too. *Joyfully. Happily. Unashamedly.* I was an artist in the making, a writer, a musician, so there would be no closet for me. There was no doubt in anyone's mind who I was, *what* I was. What I *wasn't*. By second grade, my life had become a series of confirmations of weirdness and sissyhood, so I had no hiding place. I even hated blue. Damn. What was I to do?

In middle school, I tried to sneak into a closet but failed. Only boys who could be heterosexual, whose behavior deemed them masculine, were allowed there, so I was turned away. No one wondered if I was *that way*; they wondered why I wouldn't admit it. The day I mentioned having a girlfriend, people gawked in stark incredulity and shouted, "A *what*?" But I liked girls. I found them smarter and more accepting than boys, so they made great companions for me. Why wouldn't I have been attracted to them? I had no real sexual desire for anyone—the church had forbidden it—but if I were to have risked intimacy, it certainly would've been with a girl. I didn't trust boys to honor my heart or protect our privacy. Most were fools—immature, silly, obnoxious—so I rolled my eyes and looked away from them. This made the closet off-limits for me. I wasn't a homeboy, a bruh, a nigga, so I never got invited inside. I couldn't have explained this then. All I knew was that no girl in her right mind would take me for her lover, although I didn't know why.

When I turned thirteen, my grandmother gave me a purse. Not for public use—even she wouldn't have had that—but as a place wherein I could put things and hide them from the world. Things like my diary. I'd kept it since third grade, and I wrote things far too personal to share. If anyone had read it, I would've been ruined. Names, dates, incidences would've implicated our entire community, and folks would've destroyed me. I had no doubt of that. So I hid my precious words at the bottom of one of Grandma's old pocketbooks. When I think about it now, I see how subversive she was, how far she went to save me, to keep me shielded from a cruel, cold world. She risked a lot to assure others didn't totally destroy me. She knew I'd never get a closet, but she didn't intend for me to be homeless either. Occasionally she'd say, "God made only one of you, baby, and He'll never make another. Be *yourself*! Don't worry about anyone else." She knew that if I followed her edict, it would cost me everything. She also knew that if I didn't, it would cost me more. So I chose to follow her. She said I'd been sent to show the world the love of God—the full, complete, unconditional love of God. I laughed. I hadn't even met God yet. And I wasn't sure He would like me.

At fifteen, I met a girl who I believed could love me. Her family had moved from Spartanburg, South Carolina, and since she didn't know me or my *situation*, I thought we might make a go of things. She wasn't particularly attractive, but neither was I, so that didn't matter. Her kindness, though, was a refreshing summer breeze. I could literally smell it whenever she approached. We spoke excitedly each morning, like newly minted best friends. I tried to temper my drama, so as not to give myself away, and, for a while, it worked. We spoke on the phone every day about frivolous things—movies, books, other kids—and when Dad discovered a girl in my life, he punched my shoulder playfully and said, "'Bout damn time! I knew you were all boy. I know what I raised!" Her name was Ursula. I asked if she'd be my girlfriend and she said sure. I smiled. I was on my way to a closet. But there was a problem: I had no sexual desire for her. I wanted to love her the way I loved Grandma and pretty flowers and cute bouncy brown puppies. After all, we were only fifteen, which was young in my day for anything physical.

Things were fine until Ursula took me beneath the bleachers during a football game and tried to kiss me. I didn't want to kiss her. I wanted a friend, a confidant, one who loved me for me. When I resisted, she frowned and asked, "What's wrong with you?"

I couldn't explain it. "Umm... Nothing. I just don't..."

"People said you're a faggot. I didn't believe them. I should've." She walked away. I could see it was over. My chance to fool the world had come to an end. All because I didn't want what everyone thought I should want.

I knew then I'd never live a life of acceptance and applause. I had read too many books on authenticity, freedom, and nonconformity. There was also no way I'd ever agree to fuck a girl *just because*. It felt thoughtless and abusive, and I was neither. I wouldn't smoke weed with boys in order to be one of them either. I just couldn't do it. I didn't long for inclusion among boys I didn't admire. So I dwelled at the margin. It was an uneasy existence. Any misstep could cost my life. It was a dance I had no choice but to master. And to do so alone.

Dad noticed my despair and inquired about it. He assumed I was entangled with *girl issues*, and he wanted to help. His excitement sickened me. When I told him I didn't want to kiss her, he settled into a chair and pouted. "What the hell's wrong with you, boy? Huh? Every boy wants to kiss a girl!" I hung my head. What do you say to a father who seeks your lesser self? How do you make him proud? I'm afraid you don't. You can't. He becomes like all the others—dismissed as disappointment. He told me not to bring that shit into his house, and although he never named it, I knew what he meant. Of course I knew. He stood, suddenly, towering over me with contempt, screaming profanity and judgment. I refused to cry. He would beget nothing from my heart.

After his rant, I went to Grandma's next door and wrote pages in my diary about the kind of father I would be. Or hoped to be. Little did I know that others had already erased—or mocked—the possibility of my fatherhood. They couldn't imagine how I could conceive a child, much less raise one. I believed I could. I had foreseen the whole thing. We would read together, my children and I, and pray before bed and laugh about funny things and hold hands as we blessed each meal. But with no closet, where would we live?

By junior year, others had decided—and I had grown to believe—I was hopelessly unlovable, so I set about trying to be what people desired. I traded beautiful healing words like *love* for ugly boy words like *fuck* and *muthafucka* and *nigga* and *kiss-my-ass*. People applauded and shouted praises, but I couldn't maintain the facade. Not over time. Not when my spirit longed for magical, Godly words that made my grandmother smile. So I reverted back to my original self after a while, and people shook their heads, mumbling, "I knew it. I knew it all along." I returned those ugly words, those death phrases, those demeaning monikers to the monsters who loved them. I should've kept *kiss-my-ass* though. There's a utility in that one.

I learned in college that closets are for queers who appear regular. They're *funny* too—believe me!—but they've learned the look and performance of normalcy. They've discovered how to move through the world without disturbing others' perception of them. My being, however, was a veritable discussion of possibilities and promises no one wanted to hear. My walk, my quick nervous sway, made others frown and whisper, so, no, I would get no closet. Closets were for those who could pass—boys, particularly, whose masculinity marked them "straight," whose gender performance canceled their faggothood. That wasn't me. Everything about me was a disruption, a private conversation, a parental rejection, so, no, hell no, I couldn't have a closet. I would stay out in the cold. No one wondered *if*, or considered *maybe not*, or argued *it wasn't so.* They simply looked at me sideways, grimacing at what God had done, and prayed never, ever to have a son like me. I didn't blame them. I didn't want me either. Not yet.

The privilege of the closet, I soon discovered, is the joy of sexual ambiguity. Anything can happen in the closet without others policing your behavior. It is quintessentially heteronormative space because every man whose sexuality goes unquestioned gets to be a patriarch. No one really knows what happens in the closet, but everyone assumes it to be heterosexual activity, and that alone is a kind of power. It means that if one learns gender performance well—or well *enough*—one can be assumed straight. Whether one actually *is* doesn't matter. In fact, same-gender sex is not the culprit; it's queer mannerisms that kill you. That twirling of the hand, that smiling directly into another man's eyes, that touching when emphasizing a point. That's what seals a man's sissydom. That's what, in others' eyes, revokes his manhood.

Americans work hard to construct a child's gender long before he or she knows it. We fear for the life of a queer kid. When they come along, most parents busy themselves trying to discern what happened, what went wrong, who did what to whom. This is usually before the child's sexual activity begins. If we can make him *act* like a boy, or soften her mannish ways, we rest easy. That is enough to assuage people's worry that a sissy or dyke is on the way.

However, intelligent people know that mannerisms (or the lack thereof) are not reliable signs of sexual orientation. Yet social constructs of gender and sexuality are deeply embedded in the American psyche. Because we still associate heteronormativity with power and divinity, most believe queer children will have difficult, unpleasant lives. So parents and others try to ward against it. Yet, somehow, queer children keepa comin'. They're safe—well, *safer*—if their queerness isn't obvious, meaning if they're able to perform gender normativity with any success. This is what "the closet" means: it's the hope for heteronormative behavior in soon-coming queers. *Can't you at least* act *like a boy? Will you please wear a dress for Mommy? Please? Just this once?* A child learns quickly the benefits of playing the part, and thus discovers the value of the closet as the ability to change identities at will, to put on regularity and thus avert suspicious eyes. The closet isn't about truth. It's about deception, and one's willingness to placate people's fear of his/her difference. Yet, lest I'm dishonest, let me admit that I have no judgment for people in the closet. Truth is, as a youngster, I was envious, even resentful, for I, too, would've hidden there if I could've. Yet every time I tried, I was put out.

Unlike other boys, I never got masculinity quite right. Too much sway in my hips, too much excitement in my voice, too much passion in my unrestricted embrace. I just wasn't a bona fide dude. *Why can't you act like a boy?* my father used to ask, unaware of how hard I tried. I just didn't know how. My gait felt natural to me. When I tried the patriarchal strut, my walk resembled an old man's—stiff and rigid—nothing like the smooth, easy glide I sought to emulate. I looked ridiculous, really, swinging robotic arms, moving forward with only the slightest shuffle. So I stopped trying. I also tried to suppress my penchant for drama, which was simply my personality, and that too failed miserably. I liked hugging others and smiling at strangers and crying when my heart overflowed and gathering wildflowers in the forest, but these weren't boy things. Certainly not traits that would earn me a closet. And how would I ever change if I had no closet?

I had nowhere to hide. I had friends in closets who invited me over, but they never suggested I could stay. We'd speak in public with a generic hand gesture or a head lift, but never with the joy we shared privately. I didn't object. They had achieved something I couldn't, and I didn't wish to ruin their charade. When they paraded girlfriends and newborn babes, I blinked tears of joy. They had arrived. Their scheme had worked. No one knew their secret. No one but me. And I had promised not to tell.

I had no idea, at nineteen, that I could love myself without a closet. I'd been made to believe self-worth was what others thought about you. And I knew what they thought. I was talented, but not adored. Gifted, but not glorified. Others shook their heads, as if my being had been a waste of God's time. Every Sunday, someone prayed for me, either from the pews or standing boldly before me with hands high and lifted up. I felt guilty of some crime I had not committed. But I submitted. If God was willing to change me, I was willing to be changed. Yet God never said a mumbling word. So, after years of weeping and pleading, I let others pray for me without my participation. I just stood by obediently and waited. Funny thing: they never laid hands on me. Now I know why.

As an adult, after earning a few degrees and finally meeting God, I came to understand that I didn't need a closet. I didn't even want one anymore. It's not for proud men and women who know who they are; it's for insecure people who enjoy homosexual acts without bearing the weight of the identity. The closet welcomes no "femmes," no "clockable" queens, no obvious dykes. It only houses those who honor status quo constructions of gender. I learned quickly that nail polish, even clear, bans a man from the closet. Makeup, of any amount, is a sure rejection. No sequins, no floral-patterned pants, no arched eyebrows, no fake hair, no unnecessary weeping—your mother's funeral might exempt you—no professional dancing, no love of baking—grilling is another thing—no standing with hands on hips, no large hoop earrings, no reading of romance novels—no reading of novels period—no screaming over Beyoncé, no admiration of Idris Elba (unless celebrating his *cool*), no dancing in church, no styling of hair, no tight pants, no love of women without fucking them. No, no, no. Not if one wants a closet. And I had wanted one. I had wanted one badly.

But I was too free. Freedom, in a land of bondage, is itself a kind of bondage. I had rejected the achievement of masculinity—or so others had thought—so no one had sympathy for me. Funny that so many gay men hate femmes. I'd thought that's what gay meant—a boy who acted like a girl. But I was wrong. Boys who acted like girls were sissies. Boys who liked boys but acted like boys were cool dudes. Their attraction to boys was irrelevant. Sissies were demeaned and degraded because they didn't—or couldn't—act like boys, whether they actually liked boys or not. A closet required masculinity. Even abstinence would be acceptable if accompanied by the performance of prowess. So there was no hope for me. Some men could get away with baking cookies—if they did so for their own children. Or they could weep freely—if into the eyes of a female lover. But me, I was too far gone. I bought flowers for myself and stared at their beauty. I wore beaded bracelets and matching necklaces. I had posters of Morris Chestnut, Nate Parker, and Lamman Rucker on my walls—not for sexual reasons, but because they were beautiful black men, and by admiring them, I was loving myself. Can't a man be beautiful to another man as an act of self-love? HELL NO, others screamed. Men can't be beautiful to other men. Period. Certainly not black men. We can deem each other "cool" or "aight" or "straight," meaning "acceptably attractive," but not downright *beautiful*. That word is reserved for people and things we seek to possess, to own, to devour. I learned this much too late.

If Jesus were alive today, he'd get a closet. He had no wife, no girlfriend, no kids, and he wept freely—but he also performed enough masculinity to create doubt. He "wilded out" in the temple, turning tables and shouting with vehement anger. That certainly helped. Then he carried a heavy cross up a hill—something only a real man could do. That undoubtedly sealed his heteronormativity. In fact, if we aren't careful, we celebrate Jesus precisely for the abuse he endured, as if bearing pain is the ultimate sign of masculine divinity. It's strange that more people don't wonder aloud about Jesus's sexuality, especially since, in his day, folks were practically forced to marry and procreate. Actually, by remaining unmarried, Jesus seems the only man in the whole of Nazareth who *didn't* follow established gender expectations. But whatever. The point here is that his fame, his reputation, rests upon violence. It's the only way we can praise him, the only way we can exalt him, as a single man who never had a woman. Turning water into wine isn't enough. Neither is raising the dead. These are not necessarily masculine achievements. But enduring the cross is. That's part of why church folks love that moment more than Jesus's entire life—because his gender performance at Calvary is undeniable. The act is so complete, so unsullied, so punk-less that his compassion, shown in other moments, pales in comparison to his virility on the cross. Put simply, he gets unbridled manhood because he died hard—not like some weakling who crumbled because others mocked him. No. He "bore our stripes" and "was whipped all night long." Then, much to everyone's surprise, he rolled that heavy-ass stone away—or someone else did—and got the hell outta that tomb. That was a bad dude, a pimped-out homey, although a sensitive, single one, too. Yes. He'd get a closet.

The real crime is what we've done with those who don't. I think of Baldwin and the work he did to persuade a world to love more fiercely, and I cry for him. Not because he couldn't have a closet—although he definitely couldn't—but because, ultimately, he loved us too much to want one. Scholars and readers alike laud him—this is the age of Baldwin—but most don't champion his sexuality as a prerequisite for his brilliance and unmatched insight. Dwight McBride's "Straight Black Studies" essay, published in the seminal anthology *Black Queer Studies*, certainly approaches this position. Yet few suggest that Baldwin's prophetic voice came precisely *because* he was gay—not in spite of it. I contend that his sexuality was the piece of God through which he understood the world. It was the 3D lens by which he saw the invisible. He didn't *happen* to be gay. He was sent gay by ancestors who knew we needed him. He never would've known what he knew or taught the world the nuances of race and gender except that he was gay. Yet we don't say this because we aren't proud of it. We're proud that he was black and exceptional *even though* he was gay. This means we've missed him altogether, I'm afraid.

Baldwin could've told us how to transform the black church—and thus save it for our children—if he'd had a closet from which to speak. Those are the only men the black church seems to hear. He loved the church, its music, its ethos, its ability to conjure hope in the midst of despair. He simply bemoaned that the church didn't love him. Still, even in unrequited love, he meant to save the church and its people. Each of his books speaks to church folks specifically: *Go Tell It on the Mountain*, *Giovanni's Room* (the upper room), *The Fire Next Time*, *The Evidence of Things Not Seen*, *The Devil Finds Work*, and so on. Baldwin was so deeply ensconced in the church he couldn't get away from it. He didn't want to. He wanted to transmute it, to make it anew, to refurbish it into a place where anyone of any difference could sit upon the throne. But, to the church, Baldwin was a faggot, which means he was dismissed as dramatic instead of understood as prophetic. Even by some of his own folks. As popular as Baldwin is now, he hasn't made black readers less homophobic. He has made them appreciate and separate his intelligence from his sexuality, but I've not heard of any man reading Baldwin then deciding he'd love to have a son just like him. Not *just* like him.

So Baldwin escaped into whiteness since blackness presented no closet for him. This was a deadly move, I believe, for it caused Baldwin to waste time begging white supremacy for acceptance and validation. I'm on thin ice here, and I know it. But it must be said. Had Baldwin been loved by his own people *the way he was*, he might've discovered early on that conversations about race and equality always position whites as the audience. We've lost enough time and intellectual energy begging whites to change. They're not going to. And we don't need them to—not if we discover our own cultural agency and construct our own value system. Baldwin never discovered this. Yet the problem of the black community is not white supremacy; it's black self-hatred. Either can exist without the other. Baldwin couldn't get us to self-love though because, without a closet, black folks wouldn't hear him. So he ran into the arms of those who eroticized him. He spent a lifetime preaching about and proclaiming the perils of America if it rejected him. And it still rejected him. There could be no good end to his story.

This is not to say his work or life was meaningless. Quite the antithesis, Baldwin's insight is, in fact, priceless and unmatched. Yet I do believe he was caught in an interstitial space between black rejection and white objectification. All because he was too effeminate for black folks and too black for white folks. He was the lone soul crying in the wilderness for place and context from which he might thrive, and no one seemed to welcome him fully. Not exactly as he was. And since he wasn't willing—or, more probably, able—to cower to the demands of sanctioned masculinity, he had no choice but to sing his songs in a strange land. For this reason, his self-imposed exile to France makes sense. However, the sad part is that, had he discovered his own African beauty—Baldwin always thought he was ugly—we might be freer now. But because his voice was too high, his wrist too limp, his face too dark, we didn't heed this prophet, this sissified man of God. So now we pay.

★★★

Boys without closets, irredeemable faggots, find themselves constructing new identities since they can never be men—or so they think. But this isn't true. No man, no group of men, governs manhood. No particular type of man is more *man* than another—not unless certain men, especially effeminate ones, excuse *themselves* from the pool of possibilities, and, often, that is precisely what happens. They forfeit manhood to those considered socially masculine. They yield to the belief that manhood rests most securely upon males considered performatively virile. How do I know this? Because uncloseted queer men seldom present themselves before the people as cultural examples of manhood boys should follow. They usually submit to being deviants—social irregulars who have no place in the pantheon of men. This surrender is logical. Effeminate boys don't grow into men the way the culture desires, so most never travel the long, hard road to personal agency whereby they dare present themselves as precisely what a boy ought to be. They conclude, subconsciously I believe, that *real* men are masculine while sissies are queers in recovery. Yet sissies are men, too. Wonderful, beautiful, flawed, talented, arrogant, strong, sensitive men whom we should hope our boys become. Once they realize this, they'll stop apologizing for their difference and stop hoping for a closet. People suffer and die in there.

Being uncloseted—and unclosetable—means several things. First, one must find or create his/her own social value. Sissies have no choice but to craft means of personal significance. Heteronormatives dismiss them as useless punks and bulldaggers who twirl in nightclubs and squander themselves sexually. Unfortunately, some accept this stereotyped identity. But not all. Many set about the business of fashioning lives of purpose and influence enough to "outweigh their defect." This is an uphill battle, especially since traditional categories of social worth—family, parenting, matehood, etc.—often appear off-limits to them. Instead, they dedicate their entire life's energy to becoming something the world will (hopefully) admire. And, perhaps, even honor. But they cannot simply be *good*; they must be extraordinary if the scheme is to work. Like Baldwin, they must be so exceptional that their sissyhood becomes irrelevant. It may even be forgiven—if they prove truly remarkable in their achievement. If not, many surrender to lives of loneliness and depression, believing that their sexual identity is some sort of curse. It is not. Indeed, it provides insight and analytical perspective in heteronormativity's blind spots. Too many unclosetable angels waste time and energy pleading for normalcy when abnormality is their blessing, their spiritual inheritance. It positions one to see what others have the privilege to ignore. It invites the rejected to love so fully, to embrace so completely, to live so broadly that oppressions dissolve in their presence. And that is the power of being uncloseted—that, through abandonment, through denial of normativity, one discovers the beauty of the authentic life. Having no closet, no hiding place, forces one to accept one's truth, to stand naked and unflinching in the face of fear and ridicule. This invites—and sometimes urges—one to speak truth to those in power in ways others can't. Or won't. By doing so, many of the uncloseted learn to walk through the valley of the shadow of death without fearing evil.

Actually, the uncloseted have nothing to lose. That's the irony of rejection: it frees one from believing in the safety of others' silence. Having shivered in the cold when colleagues had warm, secure closets, the uncloseted know that safety won't produce freedom fighters. It won't convince comfortable queers to surrender their privilege in exchange for brazen authenticity. It won't show people that fighting for another's freedom *IS* fighting for one's own. No. The safety of the closet blinds residents and privatizes joy. It suggests that as long as people don't know who you are, they can't hurt you. But they can. Their ignorance, their fear, can kill you. It always does because what they never tell you is that God won't dwell in a closet. God exists only in liberty, self-love, and fearless truth. God wants what God planted in you—fully bloomed and unashamed. So, it will take brave uncloseted souls—those who know, finally, firmly, *why* they're queer, *why* they're here—to help construct everyone else's freedom—and to live unsatisfied until they do.

The deadly nature of the closet is what the movie *Moonlight* is about—black men who love each other but don't have the strength to claim it. This film, released in 2016, tells the story of two black boys who, as youngsters, share private, unspoken intimacies and attractions that they never forget. In adulthood, they find themselves together again, lost in a silent matrix of magnetism, which neither has the power to overcome. Their desire is limited by "hood" doctrine, the unspoken set of laws that govern inner-city black boys' public behavior. However, their love is undeniable. The movie teases through the tensions of black male-male desirability and the ways in which masculinity imprisons it. When I exited the theater and heard folks proclaiming, "Finally! A beautiful gay love story!" I was confused. *Moonlight* doesn't champion the beauty of same-gender love; it demonstrates what men lose when they *can't* love freely. It's beautifully done. But it's not a movie about the resilience and power of gay men. It's a movie that explores same-gender attraction in heteronormative black men. In other words, the public's embrace of *Moonlight* had everything to do with the fact that the main characters *weren't* gay—not in any sissified sense. Indeed, they are so hypermasculine that their masculinity outshines their sexuality, and that, dear readers, is precisely what black America wants—men, patriarchal men, obvious men, but men dammit!—who don't disrupt their notions of acceptable male behavior. This movie is not a gay love story. It's the story of two young black men who never achieve the agency to admit and embrace their truth. The protagonists aren't even gay! Not in the truest sense. They don't love men—they're simply attracted to each other. And if being attracted to just one man makes a man gay, then every man in America is gay. Of course, this is ridiculous. Truth is, the main characters in this movie are miserable, bound and imprisoned by their own acceptance of heteronormativity and its limits. The funny, sad thing is that many black gay men lauded this film as "what we've been waiting for." But there is no liberty here, no celebration of the joys of difference. Only confirmation that most gay men hate faggots, too. It is the movie's unbridled display of hypermasculinity that leaves a few of us wondering how gay men praised it as self-celebrating. Perhaps some extolled it for exposing the emotional toll of the closet, for, indirectly, encouraging black men to love against all odds, but too many black gay men simply applauded the hope, the hint, of black male romance as if the idea alone satisfies.

One disturbing manifestation of the hypermasculinity in this film is the constant use of the word "nigga." Said in a coarse tone, the word reinforces that Kevin and Black are *not* wimps. They are not to be regarded as weak or girly or sweet. They are niggas—bruhs, homeboys, partners. When I noted this, I remembered that many gay men share this sentiment.

They, too, want bruhs, straight-acting men—not *"femmes"* who switch around like women. They want gay men with heteronormative currency—no traces of faggotry in them. It's interesting that some gay men want gayness stripped of its punkish possibilities. Actually, *Moonlight* illumines that the black community can take homosexuality—if it is cloaked in patriarchy. It's those damn queens and sissies that fuck up everything for everyone. In other words, if one can perform masculinity well enough not to shame or disgrace the people, no one cares whom you sleep with. So, in many ways, the celebration of *Moonlight* is the celebration of the closet. It's an affirmative nod to black men who love each other without forsaking the general standards of black masculinity. It's Hollywood's refusal or inability to imagine black men loving black men without constraint or socially sanctioned boundaries.

When, in their teenage years, Kevin and Black masturbate on the beach, viewers know this affair must be forever private. It can never be spoken of or lauded as a beautiful moment between lovers. Because they're not lovers—they're insecure kids whose imagination far exceeds the strength of their reality. As adults, the men avoid each other altogether until the day the urge won't be denied. Even then, their interior imprisonment is debilitating. The reunion in the café is at once magnificent and tragic, for viewers see not what they have, but what they *could have had* had they dared follow their hearts. This, I contend, is why many black gay men loved the film—because they, too, have spent a lifetime conforming and thus missed half the joy of being themselves. Yet this is not a celebration of same-gender existence! It's an illustration of what happens to same-gender-loving people who surrender their truth in exchange for the world's acceptance. I love the movie for this.

But when people exalt it as a declaration of the beauty of black male love, I understand them to be applauding the notion that at least some gay men are "real niggas" too.

Well, I ain't one of them. And I don't seek to be. Not anymore. But I am a man—and I don't need other men to agree. I find nothing about myself that requires an apology. My grandmother had been right. Thank God I didn't have a closet. I would've traded every gift within me to keep it.

INTEGRATION: A FAILED EXPERIMENT

Many elders of the civil rights movement now regret the outcome of integration. They remember nostalgically dreams of black communal and economic self-sufficiency, and some even recall plans for an independent black state. A few admit that the real hope was for equal access to goods and resources since black labor made them possible in the first place. "We had already paid for every privilege we sought," one elder told me. "We marched and fought so white folks would surrender to us what already belonged to us." But now, fifty years later, some elders question whether they did the right thing. Their assessment of what the black community lost—versus what it gained—makes most shake their heads. What they make clear is that they never hoped for peaceful reconciliation with hostile whites. Blacks were not that naive. What sense would it have made for them to believe that racism could be dismantled merely by kindness? No, they knew that social and spiritual transformation in America would require far more than a simple olive branch. What they knew best was that, in the coexistence of black and white, black always got the short end of the stick. Always. Certainly many whites sympathized with the black cause of freedom—hasn't this always been true?—but there were far more who didn't. Indeed the 1954 *Brown v. Board* federal mandate exposed precisely the attitude most whites across America held toward the possibility of black inclusion in solid white social structures. So if most Americans—white and black—were skeptical of integration, why did it occur?

Elders told me that, initially, they wanted social desegregation—not integration. But since whites didn't have the spiritual fortitude or the moral character to be both separate and equal, integration was the only option. Yet it wasn't their desire. Not by a long shot. Blacks simply hoped to be treated equally and fairly under the law. They hoped their tax money would support their own schools. They wanted the right to sit in the front of the bus—not because whites sat there, but because they had paid the same fare and wanted the right to choose where they sat. They wanted the ability to walk the streets at night without being lynched. They wanted the police to protect them too—since their tax money also paid police salaries. Yet since whites seemed unwilling to honor this basic code of ethics, black civil rights leaders were forced to plan B—integration. It is absolutely critical to note, however, that this was not what they initially desired.

This fact must not be downplayed. It reveals many hard truths about America that scholars have chosen to ignore. Or leave unspoken. Like the fact that the moral crisis in America in the 1960s was a white dilemma—not a black one. Whites and white-dominated power structures terrorized black people and communities so harshly that blacks could not sustain a peaceful living. Had whites been sufficiently kind and fair, blacks would never have needed integration, much less wanted it. In other words, the problem of the 1960s was a dilemma of white supremacy and its perpetuation. It was a struggle for absolute power that included the subordination of anyone who wasn't white. It was never a dream of the coexistence of all people; it was the commitment of white authority to assure that black people and their institutions didn't prosper. It was the use of black money, black talent, black time, and black labor in the exaltation of white social structures wherein blacks could not participate. That was the problem. If blacks could've gotten their fair share of the American pie—which they had baked *and* served—and been able to live without fear, integration probably never would have occurred.

This is a sad truth. Not about integration, but that most whites didn't have the moral fiber to treat people fairly without being forced to do so. Let's be honest: It was not blacks who threatened whites, leaving them in perpetual fear for their lives. It was not blacks who disallowed white children into publicly funded schools. It was not black people who refused to serve whites in public restaurants. It was whites whose humanity couldn't be trusted. This must be said because, otherwise, America teaches integration as having been the collective hope of a nation, the melding and unification of races and differences, when, in actuality, it was the last hope of a people who whites did not want and refused to respect.

In some ways, black activists were, in fact, naive. They were young and full of dreams, hoping in their hearts that righteous agitation would dismantle the spirit of hatred dwelling in the hearts of their fellow white citizens. King articulates such hope in "Letter from Birmingham Jail" wherein he asks white moderates to join him in the battle for social justice. He then sighs and says, "Perhaps I was too optimistic; perhaps I expected too much."

It is not difficult to imagine how black faith, groomed since the days of slavery, prepared black youth in the 1960s to invest in the spiritual transformation of a nation that had never before undergone any such thing. We had been a people whose survival depended upon faith and miracles. We were also a people who believed that all humans served the same God and therefore possessed the same potential for righteousness. In our hearts dwelled the philosophical supposition that any human, faced with overwhelming goodness, would be compelled to be good himself. Thus, with the civil rights movement, blacks set out to heal America's racial divide through nonviolent social means. The results, however, were not at all what they had hoped for.

Whites did not—certainly not immediately—surrender their color biases and yield to the way of righteousness as provoked via the lives of Fannie Lou Hamer, Ella Baker, Stokely Carmichael, John Lewis, or King himself. Instead, they became more violent. One could argue, in fact, that peaceful demonstration only incited rage and contempt in the hearts of white Americans. This was disappointing to say the least. Sympathetic whites, and there were many, appear to have been primarily on the margins of the movement—not the center. There is very little evidence—then or now—that black social agitation shifts the hearts of large sects of white Americans. On the other hand, social demonstrations did compel hundreds of thousands of blacks to join the cause of human freedom. This result definitely strengthened the civil rights movement and swelled the human tidal wave headed toward the nation's capital in the 1963 March on Washington. But the fact that white hearts, for the most part, went unchanged meant that if blacks were to improve their social and economic condition, they would have to try a new strategy.

And they did. In December of 1955, black citizens of Montgomery, Alabama, staged the most incredible and successful boycott in American history. They gathered and decided not to ride public buses until the city agreed to dismantle local laws against fair appropriation of public facilities. The city stubbornly refused. So black people walked everywhere they went or, if elderly, rode in black-owned automobiles, which many surrendered to the success of the movement. They took matters into their own hands and decided not to wait for white approval of their demands. And whites did not approve. But blacks discovered a central tenet of Fanon's theory of the oppressed—when the downtrodden get frustrated enough and realize they form the basis of the social order, they will rise up and disrupt (if not destroy) the very structures that once bound them. I stick my chest out when I read about the unity of my people during the Montgomery Bus Boycott. How black women and men orchestrated their own lives on their own terms, if only for a while. I'm proud that those buses ran up and down Montgomery streets completely empty. I'm proud that black children walked miles and miles to schools that did not excuse tardiness under the circumstances. I'm proud that black churches lent space and spiritual coverage to their own people as they strategized their own freedom. And I'm proud that although most of them were under extreme physical duress, they did not compromise their goal. Most of these people were working-class black folks. They weren't college degreed, but they were brilliant. They may not have read the latest literature, but they knew what the Bible said. They weren't wealthy, most of them, but they dreamed of living in mansions not made by hands. And they merged together to form a wall of resistance that soon became impenetrable. But all of this was necessary only because whites refused to share power—with the same people who had birthed, bathed, and buried them.

The boycott lasted just over a year. Some white liberals argue that white women played a significant role in the movement since many voluntarily (and secretively) drove black maids to and from work. And this is true. But for many, it was not because they believed in justice; rather, they believed in black hands performing their labor, regardless of a social movement. In other words, white women surreptitiously participated in the boycott in order to avoid scrubbing their own floors and cooking their own meals. This truth kept black women employed, but it also kept the hierarchies of race and class firmly rooted in Montgomery. Yet when the boycott finally ended, black people had tasted power unlike ever before. They had feasted upon the fruit of collective social resistance and taught a nation that they were not to be ignored or counted out.

Still, some sixty years later, black elders from that generation are not proud of what black communities look like these days. They do not believe popular cultural productions, such as hip-hop, reinforce the values they fought to preserve. To be sure, they do not regret the attempt to make America heterogeneous; indeed, they believe that all people, regardless of color, ought to coexist and mutually prosper in a land with unlimited resources. This was their dream. Yet a critical review of the state of black America since integration reveals that the hope of black prosperity, alongside white supremacy, never occurred for the masses of black people. Actually, many elders weep because several social gains achieved prior to the 1970s were gambled and lost in the move toward integration.

For instance, in the 1950s and '60s, segregated black communities boasted and supported black businesses, which in turn economically undergirded their constituency. Black grocery stores, hardware suppliers, meat markets, auto dealers, mechanics, seamstresses, shoe repairmen, cleaners, and the like prospered because of the support of their own. In many instances, black middle-class citizenry rose from the ranks of these small business owners and created an elite class of African Americans who became the pride of a people happy to find, in black form, the social equivalent of white privilege. The black dollar was turned over enough times in the black community to keep black folks away from a crippling dependence on whites. Now, however, once-thriving black communities are filled with abandoned (or regentrified) buildings, mere relics of bygone days of black collective economic strength. Of course blacks had the option to continue supporting black businesses even after integration, yet this social rearrangement invited their money elsewhere. In truth, the allure of association with whiteness drew many away from their own economic center, while others abandoned black-owned businesses for the convenience and cheaper prices white competition offered. In and of itself, this freedom to shop wherever one chooses is the blooming of a free market society, one wherein consumer choice is a social virtue. The problem with integration, however, is that whites never entered the realm of choosing. In other words, when given the option, whites, practically without exception, did not choose to spend their money with black businesses, regardless of the quality (often the superiority) of the product. The white dollar rarely found its way into black cash registers although the black dollar made white cash registers sing. Integration was supposed to make everyone share with everyone and allow every community to enjoy its own economic sovereignty. This did not happen.

The education of black children was another gamble lost in the crap game called integration. Segregated black schools across the nation educated, loved, and nurtured black children when white Americans didn't care if black children could read or not. An ignorant black populace was advantageous to a white society that needed black servitude for its underpinning. Yet poor, often dilapidated black schools turned the tide of black social imprisonment by educating those who otherwise would never have tasted the sweet nectar of knowledge. Against the odds, teachers planted seeds of opportunity and self-worth in the minds of children deemed worthless. These teachers knew that an educated people could never be enslaved again. They gave their lives to ensure this truth, often teaching for little or nothing but the hope for a day when black children could not be denied. These foresighted jegna surrendered the use of their shoulders to children desperate for jobs other than those of domestics, field hands, and preachers. According to the testimony of those who attended these fragile institutions, black teachers cared for and groomed the entire child—their character as well as their intellect. These teachers were among the very few who had attained education (and, for some, college degrees) only because they were either too brilliant to be rejected or because families saved every possible penny to educate just one. That one child understood his/her obligation to the people, and those who returned as classroom instructors gave, according to testimony, everything they had to lift the veil of ignorance from an entire population. These were segregated schools, with outdated books, almost no budget, no PTA, and minimal, if any, taxpayer dollars. Attendees speak of these schools with nostalgic pride, not because they were perfect or well-maintained, but because teachers believed in excellence and disallowed mediocrity.

Integration compromised this standard. Black children were bused to schools where narrow-minded educators did not share their former teachers' convictions concerning the importance of education for blacks. They sat in classrooms with hostile peers and prayed for the school day to end that they might return to those who loved them. Many testify that the academic rigor in white schools paled in comparison to that of black schools. Nonetheless, black students adjusted and proved themselves the intellectual equal and often superior of their white comrades. What was insulting was the suggestion, indeed the public declaration, that their schools had been inferior by design and consequently produced subpar scholars. This is illustrated by the fact that black children were bused to white schools, although white children were never (for the most part) bused to black schools. Supposedly, white schools were structurally superior and thus capable of accommodating black students whereas black schools could not return the favor.

The real issue, however, was that public tax dollars, those of black and white citizens, disproportionately funded the building and maintenance of segregated white schools, and black parents desired for their children the same educational opportunities their tax dollars had bought white kids. Certainly if black schools had received their fair share of public funds, the thought of shipping black children into hostile white territory would have been laughable. Unfortunately, however, the real laughable thing was the idea of equal distribution of public funds, so apprehensive black parents picketed and prodded the US government to force local municipalities to allow black children into educational facilities their parents' money had paid for. The shame here was that the excellence of Negro schools went unacknowledged. Had at least some white students been mandated into black schools, the integrity of integration could have been realized. As it was, the worth and value of black social institutions were so insulted as to suggest that they could not accommodate the needs of whites. Not only was this untrue, but the reality that white students never submitted to the tutelage of black instruction simply reinforced their own assumed superiority and undoubtedly made them believe, as did many blacks, that black schools and, by extension, black institutions were inherently inferior.

No wonder black elders of the preintegration era reminisce with pride about an academic experience few contemporary children will ever know. Even in substandard physical conditions, with teachers who earned half that of their white counterparts, black children learned and felt good about themselves. With integration, even if they still learned, feeling good about themselves became a thing of the past.

The greatest price of integration was the deterioration of a cohesive black community. Not in the ideological sense, but quite literally the crumbling of black neighborhoods and townships that once housed the collective consciousness and culture of a people. Said differently, with integration came the notion not simply that blacks *could* leave their communities but in fact that they *should*. The ability to live in someone else's neighborhood, where property values were higher and schools "better" became the sign and symbol of black social progress. Of course colored neighbors soon discovered that their entry meant whites' exit, and with the latter went all social privilege blacks had hoped to attain. In many instances, white affluent neighborhoods became black practically overnight. Apparently whites could not envision the maintenance of their privileged status alongside black citizens. Nonetheless, the real tragedy is not the unsolicited infiltration of white communities by black hopefuls, but the abandoning of black homes, churches, and schools by those who now regret having left them. Every major city in America is home to historic black neighborhoods where the brightest of our people once dwelled. This is true for rural areas as well. Homecoming events in the country often mark the return to once-thriving settlements that had everything a community ever needed. Still, we left them, believing that urban centers offered a quality of life greater than any we had achieved. By the time we realized this wasn't so, we had sold or simply walked away from our inheritance. Now it's gone forever.

Again, this question: Why didn't whites move into black neighborhoods? And again, the answer: because they never believed black communal space offered anything they needed. Integration was the supposed elevation of blacks to the status of white Americans. The latter were already superior, most believed. This, plus their disproportionate control over America's resources, made them the measure of excellence to which minorities should aspire. But this is not what integration should've been! Integration is the merger of equal or complementary parts such that, in the end, neither exists solely as itself. We know that America did not integrate. Certainly not fully. Yes, many were forced to coexist and countless white neighborhoods became black, but there was no merger of equally valued parts. In fact, disenfranchised blacks still had to fight their way into white spaces much to the latter's chagrin. Had whites been forced to know the beauty and value of African American life and culture the way blacks knew whiteness, true integration might have occurred.

It is important to clarify that blacks' desire for the goods and resources of whites was not simply because whites had it. General testimony of the era assures that most blacks did not admire white privilege above the beauty of black culture. They simply sought the lifestyle they felt they had earned. Yet the more they fought to have it, the more they were denied it, until the hope of equality deteriorated into an obsession with whiteness that has now become black cultural pathology. And since, in America, race cannot be spoken of honestly or directly for fear of offense or revelation of people's private truth, black need for white validation continues and functions as a relic of a soiled social system that never intended the true coexistence of difference to begin with.

Still, I assert that integration was not a bad idea in theory. In fact, it was a noble prospect, a social inevitability, which needed to come. What should've happened was the empowering of black social spaces first so that everyone—black and white—saw the value of black people and their institutions before forcing them to uphold the sanctity of whites and theirs. Then, at least some whites would've voluntarily moved into black communities as blacks moved into theirs. Some blacks would've sent their children to predominately white colleges, which they did, and some whites would've sent their children to predominately black colleges, which they did not. This is the face of true integration.

What actually happened in America is a social travesty. In

order to access equal resources, blacks had to join white social institutions, which means that blacks had to perpetuate the idea of white supremacy, although that's not what they meant to do. The repercussions, however, were devastating. We began to sing praises of those who simply "got in" to white institutions as if the entry itself were divine. To be the "first black" to do a thing is only significant because it occurred before a white audience. The first black graduate of a white school is celebrated because whites now have no choice but to acknowledge that student's intelligence. Truth is, blacks graduated from extraordinary black schools long before these so-called "first black" achievements ever occurred. But this is an outcome of the forced entry of blacks into white spaces. We celebrate simply that we got in—not the worth of what we did or found inside.

Put bluntly, many whites and blacks, it seems, began to believe that the legitimacy of black achievement occurred only under the supervision of blue eyes. This is critical to understand, for shifting black talents and resources into white spaces assured the crumbling of black institutions. Integration deluded black people (and white people) into believing that black presence in white spaces is a black achievement. Boasting of one's entry and matriculation through, say, a white elite college is a prime example. If I've heard it once, I've heard it a thousand times: "Du Bois was the first black PhD graduate from Harvard University!" But is this Du Bois's achievement or Harvard's? And why is this an achievement at all? Because most blacks didn't do it? Because people think most blacks *couldn't*? This is a mental psychosis that needs immediate correction. It gives credit of black sweat to white institutions that *"allowed"* our ancestors' presence! For instance, why isn't Du

Bois's brilliance, his academic achievement, accredited first to Fisk University? That's where his intellectual foundation was laid. In fact, I daresay that Harvard was probably easier. The standard and academic expectation of HBCUs in Du Bois's day was second to none! I'm clear that Fisk's foundation made Du Bois's Harvard days possible. Yet people speak of Du Bois's attendance at Harvard as practically surreal. This is the sickness blacks have carried since the days of integration. And many whites agree.

The list of black "firsts" is longer than the Mississippi River. It's almost always in relationship to some white institution. Black excellence didn't start with integration, but the *recognition of it* juxtaposed to whiteness became a cultural celebration during that era. Said differently, boasting of black achievement in white spaces during the 1960s became a way of convincing whites that black people were worthy of their presence. Blacks already knew of their own hard work and excellence. That was no secret. It was white folks we were trying to convince of our merit. This soon became a social fixation. Now, if you google "black firsts," a list of achievements surfaces that makes black people seem supernatural—instead of simply presenting us as keepers of an excellence tradition that started long before whites recognized it or welcomed it in their ranks. That's the problem with this "first black" nonsense—it credits the place of the achievement instead of the person.

Take, for another instance, the immeasurable literary achievement of Toni Morrison. No one has stretched the American imagination like she has, and no one has produced an oeuvre so complicated, so brilliant, that countless scholars devote their entire careers to studying her work. But very few praise Howard University as the incubator of her intelligence. If it were a white school, it would get all the glory. People mention Howard in her biography, but they don't wonder of the nature of her professors who must've known and taught literature and literary analysis like few others. It's as if she went to Howard but gained no intellectual transformation there, as if she arrived as brilliant as she ever would be. This was not true. She couldn't have achieved such literary heights had she not been trained by the likes of Sterling Brown and Charlotte Watkins and Owen Dodson. However, no one is looking for these figures in history because few understand or even believe that they were greater intellectually than the students they produced.

I understand this phenomenon firsthand. People ask me incessantly where I did my PhD, yet, without doubt, my undergraduate years at Clark College were just as difficult, just as stretching of my imagination. Temple University's African American Studies faculty—Sonia Sanchez, Molefi Asante, Kariamu Welsh, Sonja Peterson-Lewis, Charles Fuller, Bobby Seale, Nate Norment, etc.—did a fine job shaping my consciousness into a self-loving, self-knowing thing; however, if I, one day, am found worthy of public recognition, the faculty of Clark College must be acknowledged first. Whatever I achieved in Temple's brand-new PhD program in African American Studies in the late 1980s must be attributed to the outstanding teaching and training provided at a little black college in Atlanta, Georgia. I am who I am because black professors planted me and raised me and grew me up. I did very well at Temple University, but not because of Temple University. I did well because Clark College gave me tools so sharp, so well crafted, that I had only to apply them, and that's what I did. Like Du Bois, I received a PhD quite young—twenty-six—but few marvel of the peculiar genius of my undergraduate professors who prepared—and expected—me to do so. And I wasn't exceptional. Many students at Clark College were far sharper than me; in fact, as a member of the honors program, I felt quite ordinary and, in several instances, inadequate. I *became* exceptional when I left home—and entered a world that was surprised at (and celebratory of) what folks at home thought commonplace.

Ultimately, with pseudo-integration, we probably lost far more than we gained. It was a valiant notion, to be sure, and a marvelous idea—the dream of national harmony between races—but most people—black and white—were suspicious of it, so the attempt occurred under extreme duress and resistance. Black people were willing to have it if whites would honor the terms, but they wouldn't, so America found itself at a racial standstill. Even now, white supremacy stands its ground as many blacks remain jaded about race relations in this country. Truth is, America is probably as integrated as it's ever going to be. With Obama came the hope of racial healing, but the ascension of Trump dissolved much of that hope. Yet, regardless, today's black youth aren't going to march nonviolently to claim their rights in this land. Those days are gone. They'll either leave America altogether or there'll be fire next time.

MASSA, DON'T LEAVE ME!

Trump won the presidency, a friend called, know- distraught I'd be, and asked, "What we gon do now, k?"

I told him, "I don't know. I really don't know."

He said, "This some deep shit, man."

"Yeah, it is," I confirmed. We chatted a while longer, then I said, "You know what? We'll survive this. We've had racist presidents before. Hell, that's 'bout all of 'em!"

We laughed uneasily. Neither of us had much confidence in the future of America. We were scared, but we were also angry. I offered, "We might just need to get the hell outta here."

He hushed abruptly. Of course I was joking—sort of—but the prospect disturbed him greatly. "We ain't got shit, man," he slurred. "So where we goin'? You feel me?"

"Where we goin'?" I shouted. I didn't feel him. "We got things, man. Black people gotta lotta stuff. We're powerful, creative people. We ain't no bankrupt community. Not by a long shot."

He chuckled. "Coulda fooled me."

I frowned. "What chu talkin' 'bout, dude? We built America from the ground up. Hell, it's rich and prosperous because of us!"

"That's 'cause they MADE us do it!" he d

"What? No, it ain't! We had civilizations
before they dragged us here."

He sucked his teeth.

I added, "You don't think black people could h
nation of our own now?"

At first, he didn't answer. Then he mumbled, "
I wouldn't go."

I couldn't believe what he was saying. "What?

"'Cause black people don't stick together. We do
each other. All we do is fight."

I gasped audibly. "You kiddin' me, right? You don't be
that, man, do you?"

"I'm sorry," he confessed, "but I do. I just wouldn't go. You
can if you want to, but I wouldn't."

My mouth hung open. "Are you crazy, bruh? A black country, government, schools, churches, everything! Hell yeah, I'd go!"

"Okay, but it'd be a lotta crime, too." That's when I hung up and paced the floor, infuriated. A black man had said this nonsense to me? How many other black people felt this way? Only when I settled did I see the lesson: black self-hatred is more lethal than any enemy black people have.

It comes in many forms. Like the branches of a mighty tree, it stretches in every conceivable direction, and no black person has ever avoided it altogether. Many will reject my idea from the start, and that's okay. But truth is, it's obvious to those who actually love being black. I won't try to explain each manifestation, for that would be impossible, yet I will give a few examples to demonstrate how black self-loathing undermines and, often, sabotages black social progress.

★ ★ ★

Let me start here: The most poignant manifestation of black self-hatred is some black people's skepticism of black unity. It is ubiquitous, this doubt that black people can actually sustain themselves and have joy and safety while doing it. Subconsciously, it's the belief that white people govern the universe and thus possess the requisite knowledge and power to sustain all life. It's fear that, if white people disappear, life as we know it will vanish. Does this sound ridiculous? Consequently, these same black skeptics seek nothing more earnestly than their association with whiteness. In fact, many of my people want simply the black version of white privilege. We want expensive cars, Italian suits, and homes filled with exquisite European furniture. The argument is "I've worked hard enough to have what I want." Or "what's wrong with nice things?" The problem, of course, is what we pay for these things—and I don't mean financially. We give our life's energy to proving that we're worthy of material comfort, when, actually, that comfort does no work in the fight for black freedom. But we do it because we've dreamed of it. And we've dreamed of it because our captors had it. For centuries, in fact, we've watched whites enjoy material possessions as most of us lived in relative poverty. Yet what we fail to realize is that, while they prospered economically, they deteriorated spiritually. The irony of America's unimaginable wealth is that white people went morally bankrupt to get it. And if black people aren't careful, we're not far behind.

Let me say this another way: social equality, too often, has meant black people's ability to mimic white existence. This, I argue, is a form of black self-hatred because it erases black agency and values counterproductive white social standards.

It's almost as if we believe that acquiring material things insults white sensibility and thus works as a kind of cultural revenge that makes black people stick their chests out to say, "You thought I couldn't have it, didn't you? I showed you!" But what do we have to prove? Why do we compare our schools to their schools? Why do we strut around in Armani suits with Michael Kors handbags as if simply having them is an achievement? Some say, "I just like these things. What's wrong with that?"

The answer lies in the basis of our aesthetic truth, and that truth is that we have not yet learned to love African cultural manifestations enough to bear them proudly. Most often when people see American blacks in, say, dashikis and kufis, they think *they're into that African stuff.* But how ridiculous is it for Africans not to bear the cultural markers of their own inheritance? No one marvels that an American white man who has never been to Italy sports a nice Italian suit. This makes sense because of his assumed cultural center. Yet when an African American dresses in traditional garb, other African Americans believe him or her to be some radical adjutant who hates white people. Of course this is absurd. But the point is how black people sometimes justify the avoidance of all things African simply by declaring that "I don't have to wear dashikis to be African." And this is true! But why wouldn't Africans want to? We think it's just a matter of choice, of aesthetic preference, but it's more complicated than that. Subconscious black desire springs from an orientation to mimic those whose materiality we admire. And since we don't see Africa or Africans as models of excess and power, we chase white capitalist manifestations with every breath we breathe—without remembering that this thrust dragged us here in the first place.

Interestingly enough, many—I daresay *most*—blacks in America have not yet agreed we're even African. We've been called many things—colored, black, Negroes, Afro-Americans—but nothing we decided upon ourselves. When someone suggests we simply call ourselves Africans, many resist, arguing that "I've never been to Africa!" or "I don't know which tribe I came from," as if either truly matters. We are Africans if we agree to be Africans. We are Africans because our ancestors are Africans. We are Africans because Africa is our homeland. We would call ourselves Africans if we were proud of Africa, but that's the dilemma. Most blacks in America know so little about Africa or African history that they can't imagine its glory. Hence, they struggle to attach themselves to it. They want an American identity because of America's international reputation of affluence and political domination. They also want America because, as everyone knows, we built it. But that—the desire to own one's place of bondage—is also pathological. It makes one obsessed with revenge and destroys creative energy. It undoubtedly feels like an achievement to, one day, purchase the place of one's servitude, but let's consider this for what it is: a subconscious admiration of whiteness.

Without basic knowledge of self, far too many black people spend their entire lives seeking ways to piss white folks off. This is why we fight so hard to invade their institutions. For decades, blacks—the exceptional ones, I daresay—have been celebrated for penetrating places where they were not wanted. We boast of black managers in white factories and black CEOs in white corporations and black politicians where they don't usually exist. We sing the praises of black families that live in opulent white neighborhoods, which most thought they couldn't afford. Never mind that they aren't wanted there. It's the fact that they *can* be there that we applaud. Obama's presence in the White House is one such example. So many black folks shouted and danced, not because of Obama's policies or convictions, but because of the pride they had that a black man could actually *be* in the Oval Office. An elder shook his head and told me, "Can you believe those little black girls are gonna be runnin' round in the *White House*?" His pride was palpable. I shook my head. That's when I realized that our collective support of Obama was not because of who he was, but because of what he represented—the symbolic elevation of a black body to the highest position in the land. Obama's ascension seemingly confirmed that black people *really are*, finally, equal to whites.

Yet the *need* for such recognition exposes what we as black people think of ourselves. It's further displayed in our perpetual use of the term *nigga.* This is a sure sign of black self-contempt. It's a hot topic, to be sure, as many fight to explain why *nigga* is okay in certain instances. Some say, "It's a term of endearment." Others say, "We've taken the word and flipped it so that now it belongs to us." Still others shrug and say, "It ain't that deep. It's just a word." Rappers have made it the central trope, arguably, of hip-hop music. Indeed, *nigga* is pumped into the consciousness of American youth a thousand times a day, and most seem unmoved. I, however, find it problematic. Even frightening. How ironic—and sad—that some black people need (or take) this demeaning, degrading term and attempt to use it for endearment, as a way to say *I love you.* I say *attempt* because, from all evidence, it does not work. The word *nigga* does not endear black hearts. It does not create respect and honor among black people, especially in strife or disagreement. It does not inspire us to love one another or fight in each other's best interest. It does not make black men think twice before striking each other. It does not excite black men about honoring black women. It does not inspire black women's sometimes hesitant voices. It does not reinforce black children's self-worth. It does not make us imagine God as ourselves. Actually, the word *nigga*, I contend, makes us hate being black. It sounds charming sometimes, the way we use it, but its effects are destructive. Whenever black men fight, the word *nigga* is employed to assist in the humiliation. "Kiss my ass, nigga!"

"Fuck you, nigga!"

"You ain't shit, nigga!"

These disgraceful phrases announce our zero value for each other. And ourselves.

It's even worse when a brother deems another *my* nigga. This possessive determiner is far too reminiscent of slavery to sit well with me. It seems to position black men as masters who also share the seeming privilege and power of human ownership. On a subconscious level, this greeting—"What up, my nigga?"—also seemingly serves to remind black men of their caste position in American society. It seems to say, "We are niggas together" and thus brothers. Yet this is a brotherhood I can do without. It's the crabs-in-a-barrel mentality, the fear that "in case you think you're more than me, let me assure you we're both just niggas." This is not the conscious use of the word, but it's the function, because *nigga* humiliates without permission. It diminishes without sanction. It destroys the imagination. The use of "my" further denigrates others by inviting them into a false unity that ultimately reifies black bondage.

The most obvious—and, in some ways, telling—sign of

black self-rejection is the names we give our children. This is critical to note because this seed of black aversion was planted centuries ago, yet it continues to bloom in black communities all over this land. I never paid much attention to it until I saw *Roots* in the 1970s—a movie that illustrated, among other things, the traumatic experience of an enslaved African boy losing his name. I was ten or so and excited to watch what promised to be the first black family saga on American television. Every evening I rushed home from school, did my chores, and waited to see what became of Kunta Kinte. During one episode, a mean white slave owner beat him for refusing to accept the name "Toby." I cried. I cried because his name meant everything to him. He'd been stolen from his village, his people, his world, and his name was his last possession. It reminded him that he was *not* a slave. I prayed he wouldn't relinquish it, but he had no choice. They were fully prepared to destroy him if he didn't. And when he did, dripping with blood on the whipping post, I shook my head and sighed. I didn't fully comprehend then the magnitude of his loss, but I *felt* it. It was as if someone had severed his arm or leg. Only then did I know the power of an African name. And I wanted one. No, I wanted *mine.* I looked like Kunta Kinte, so I believed I had an African name somewhere. It seemed right that I would. After all, my people, too, were taken from Africa and dragged to this New World. My mother had named me Daniel, and I understood the significance. I'd read the story in the Bible and appreciated the trials young Daniel endured and the ways he distinguished himself. Still, I knew Daniel wasn't my name. Not my real name. My real name was older than the Bible and created by people who knew a black God. That was the name I wanted. That was the name I meant to find. Watching *Roots* taught me how non-African names diminish African flesh, and, although I couldn't have explained it then, my yearning for an African identity sprouted and has never waned since. As an adult, I found, finally, my ancestral name—Omotosho—and it has made all the difference in my understanding of who I am and why I exist.

However, for the sake of survival, enslaved Africans stopped giving children African names. This was devastating, and the results have shaped black consciousness for the last four hundred years. Trying not to die, we've abandoned most African traditions—including the naming process—and thus given our children names of our oppressors. This is pathological, certainly, but it's so common as to appear normal. In fact, today, giving a black child an African name appears revolutionary. At the root of this complex, layered social dilemma lies the truth that most African Americans are light-years away from any African identity. We don't see ourselves as African, define ourselves as Africans, or want to be African—although most black people look African. Instead, because of the desire to share the spoils of capitalism, we name our children after white folks, hoping that such an identifier will assist their movement toward material success. And it might. But it won't make them love themselves. Or keep America from killing them. Just ask Martin or Malcolm or Medgar. Or, more recently, Sandra or Trayvon or Michael Brown or Eric Garner or Freddie Gray. European names did not save them either.

An African American child with an African name is sure to be mocked and derided, as if the name were a joke. It will be black people, no doubt, who inspire this ridicule, believing, perhaps subconsciously, that the Middle Passage birthed them anew and thus severed forever their tie to the African continent. Therefore, to give a black child an African name seems almost ridiculous since they have no ideological or cultural allegiance to the motherland. This, of course, is the problem—the notion that black people can be understood outside of the context of their African origins. This is how and why some scholars begin the teaching of black history with slavery. But that's another story. For this point, suffice it to say that many black folks want to be American, and American only, because this assures their inclusion in the legacy of the American dream. We call our children Charles and Anthony and Sarah and Matthew and Darrell and Billy and Lisa and Elizabeth and Mark because, subconsciously, we revere white supremacy and its traditions. Names like Chisanganda and Alatanga and Kwabena and Ayodele and Oluremi and Wole are as foreign to most black folks as Mars. And in their imaginations, these names carry no meaning, no weight, no authority because those who bear them seemingly have no influence in the world. So we go on naming our children after those who despise us. No wonder we despise ourselves, too.

For a minute, during the revolutionary Black Arts Movement of the 1960s, conscious-minded black folks assumed the agency to name themselves. Many surrendered Western names in exchange for names that connected them to a legacy and past far older than slavery. LeRoi Jones became Amiri Baraka; Don L. Lee became Haki Madhubuti; Stokely Carmichael became Kwame Ture; Paulette Williams became Ntozake Shange; Cassius Clay became Muhammad Ali; Malcolm X became El-Hajj Malik El-Shabazz; and so on. I understand this act now more than ever. It didn't make them more African; it made them creators of their own destinies, lovers of their past and futures, good or bad. The trend was popular in the '60s, but it didn't hold, undoubtedly because African names didn't go well with Eurocentric mentalities. Still, the thrust was toward self-love. Those names might've kept us from killing each other over the past fifty years. Names have that kind of power, you know.

The last, though most insidious, sign of black self-rejection is our embracing of someone else's imagination. I say "our embracing" because I do not accept the notion that black people possess no agency. Yes, we were once enslaved, and, yes, we still live in a land of anti-blackness, but this does not mean we cannot fight for governance of our own mental faculties. I refuse to believe our social condition fully inhibits our ability to dream. Not now. Perhaps this was true fifty years ago. Perhaps it was true for four hundred years. But it's not true now. Black ancestors died so it wouldn't be true. Some ran to freedom, others ran to libraries, others ran to Congress to assure that, one day, black children could think for themselves and create the quality of life they desired. That day has come.

I am not suggesting that the social dilemma facing black people has somehow disappeared. Rather, I believe that freedom is the ability to construct the terms of one's life, regardless of the difficulties one faces. The irony is that, from the looks of things, the longer we stay in America, the more enslaved we become. Nat Turner *chose* freedom although he knew it would cost him everything. Harriet Tubman *chose* freedom even though slave catchers chased her a lifetime; Frederick Douglass constructed freedom by speaking truth even though whites hated him for it; Shirley Chisholm ran for president in the 1970s because she believed she could lead the nation—whether others agreed or not. These ancestors knew something about themselves, their people, that didn't require white authorization. Nowadays, practically everything black people do contains the query of what white folks think about it. And, often, our fear of their retaliation dismantles our commitment to the project.

However, this fear is certainly well-founded. America has proven its willingness to destroy black creativity and the people who spawn it. Yet even this doesn't mean we shouldn't do it. There would never have been a black Wall Street if we had lived in fear of white retribution. Whatever they tear down we have the skills, talents, and intelligence to build again—if our imagination were not incarcerated. I think of ants who build fragile structures of loose dirt. All of us have destroyed an ant mound before, but all they do is build it again. They waste no time trying to reprimand the destroyer. They know they are creators, and they never forget it. They are small, seemingly insignificant, and, compared to other life forms, powerless. Yet their strength is in their unity, their clarity that nothing, ultimately, can ruin their might.

In other words, they never lose their imagination of themselves. This is the greatest hindrance to black social and spiritual progress in America—our desire for the oppressor's spoils in exchange of our ingenuity. Most of what we want, what we dream of, is what white folks have. When we think of founding a black school, for instance, we dream of black children playing rugby and quoting Socrates—not sitting with trees until they learn to communicate with them. We don't envision black children studying the spiritual system of the Dogon in order to know the dimensions of time travel. This is because our imagination is as enslaved as our bodies once were. This reality makes us adore and admire everyone except ourselves.

The famous historian Baba John Henrik Clarke wrote a

classic story titled "The Boy Who Painted Christ Black." It's beautifully written yet hardly ever anthologized, and you can guess why. The story is set in the 1940s or so, and Aaron Crawford, the brilliant Negro boy protagonist, is the shining star of the local Negro school. He is also black—coal black. The narrator says, "His skin was so solid black that it glowed, reflecting an inner virtue that was strange, and beyond my comprehension." This is significant because Aaron's dark skin contrasts with his exceptional intelligence. He is not supposed to be smart because he's so very black. But in fact his darkness catapults his search for inner beauty, inner divinity, and he finds it in his imaginative rendering of a black Christ figure. The boy paints this picture as a gift to his art teacher, who, at first, is a bit startled, but then slowly understands exactly the kind of insight he has inspired in the child. The teacher makes the fatal decision to display this masterpiece at the school's commencement exercises where the white superintendent will be in attendance. When he sees the portrait, displayed as the centerpiece of the Negro school's achievement, he asks, "Who painted this sacrilegious nonsense?" Aaron speaks up and says, "I painted it, sir." The crowd freezes because it fears white disapproval. Negroes know that such an act could cost the boy his life. And the future of their school. So they tremble as they prepare to hear the white superintendent's response. Of course he is enraged. He fires the teacher but not before Aaron explains, "Th' principal said a colored person have jes' as much right paintin' Jesus black as a white person have paintin' him white." The superintendent is mortified. The teacher speaks up for himself and Aaron: "I encouraged the boy in painting that picture," he said firmly. "And it was with my permission that he brought the picture into this school." The teacher continues: "I don't think the boy is so far wrong in painting Christ black. The artists of all other races have painted [God to look like them]. I see no reason why we should be immune from that privilege." This declaration seals the teacher's fate and sends him off, packing his bags. But Aaron has discovered something: if black people are bold enough, they can change their own reality. White disapproval is irrelevant in the face of black self-love. The teacher finds another job at another Negro school and takes Aaron with him to complete his apprenticeship. Neither bears sorrow nor regret. Only pride that they dared to imagine themselves holy. And it will take this audacity, this risky fearlessness, to explode the boundaries of hatred that black people have embraced for hundreds of years.

The point here is that black self-hatred is real and deeply rooted in the black American psyche. Everything from colored contact lenses to hair weaves and do-rags often argue for rejection of the black self. Terms like "good hair" mean that most black hair is objectionable—nappy, kinky, and coarse. Few think of these things consciously; yet when one does, it becomes apparent that many black people's imaginations are clouded by our desire to be somebody else. I understand the seed of this desire. There is no judgment here. Yet I also understand that in order to love ourselves fully and freely, we must uproot this seed and plant a crop of black joy and black love, black self-respect and black divinity in our hearts. Only this harvest will feed us. Only this harvest will sustain us. Only this harvest will keep us from begging for self-worth from people who never meant for us to have it.

HARRIET'S CHARIOT

In recent decades, black women filmmakers have exploded with earth-shattering productions that demonstrate the difference a black woman makes behind the camera. Julie Dash's *Daughters of the Dust* (1991), Maya Angelou's *Down in the Delta* (1998), Gina Prince-Bythewood's *Love and Basketball* (2000), Beyoncé's *Lemonade* (2016), Dee Rees's *Mudbound* (2017), Melina Matsoukas's *Queen & Slim* (2019), and Chinonye Chukwu's *Clemency* (2019) all demonstrate that black women have a storytelling mode that reaches beyond the limits of patriarchy and extends the voice of a people to include the marginalized and the ignored. Indeed, black women filmmakers have detonated the boundaries of black narratives such that LGBTQ stories as well as little-known historical accounts of important black people are now part of contemporary black visual culture. Yet nothing, in my estimation, exceeds the brilliance and creative prowess of Kasi Lemmons's historical biopic *Harriet.* The film is a cinematic masterwork, a marvel of imagination, a spiritual homage to a black woman who sacrificed everything to save her people. It is so nuanced, so culturally centered, so unapologetically transcendent that I sat in the theater watching it in awe. Harriet Tubman came alive for me.

The difficulties of her life, juxtaposed against her resilience and spiritual fortitude, showed her as one who loved freedom enough to die—and kill—for it. I knew her story, of course, before I saw the film, but after the film, I knew her heart.

Controversy around the movie swirled prior to its release. Many viewers disparaged the choice of Cynthia Erivo, a British African, as the main character because of her unfavorable remarks concerning African Americans. Others wrestled with the historical inaccuracy of certain details in the story. Still others bemoaned the antagonistic role of Bigger Long, the black male slave catcher whose financial greed drives his continuous search for Harriet. Yet he was believable to me. Money has always been enough to motivate a few black folks to sell their souls. But it was Harriet who captured my consciousness. Her willingness to risk everything, even her own family, to forge a pathway to freedom for enslaved black people made me honored to be in her lineage.

Then, as I drove home, I realized something else: the movie displays African spirituality unlike anything I'd seen. Somehow, Lemmons tells Harriet's story through the lens of Ifá—the Yoruba spiritual system that many enslaved Africans brought to the New World. Its home is Southwest Nigeria—the birthplace of Erivo herself. This is no coincidence. Actually, it undergirds my belief that invisible forces participated in this artistic creation. *Harriet* is an offering to diasporic Africans, a visual reminder of their priceless spiritual inheritance. Such a gift could come only from one who understands African spirituality the way Lemmons obviously does.

In essence, Ifá teaches the value of nature, the importance of ancestors and elders, and the ways in which energy is transferred and manipulated through divine deities known as orisha. Ifá argues that all things are ultimately connected and, in fact, orchestrated for each person's higher, greater good. The deities or orisha that govern the universe have a vested interest in people for reasons of their destinies. Harriet Tubman was no exception. Her life's calling invited these deities who then lent their powers unto her in order that she might free her people. Kasi Lemmons elucidates such in this film, and perhaps it is this spiritual experiment that makes the film so exceptional—and visually resplendent.

I attended this movie with members of the Nation of Ndugu and Nzinga—a society of black folks in Atlanta who study and create African traditions. We shouted, screamed, and wept because everything we've studied materialized on-screen: The importance of submission to God and elders, the sanctity of nature, the utility of mystical knowledge, and the critical need to know one's gift and calling. We've also surveyed Ifá, to varying degrees, and therefore recognized immediately Kasi Lemmons's use of its tenets. Such a syncretic display of African spirituality in American popular culture, even black American popular culture, is virtually nonexistent. However, the ideation of African traditions and beliefs is so integrated with the life of Harriet Tubman that such a display cannot be ignored. Kasi Lemmons, whether intentional or not, has transmuted Harriet Tubman's story into a saga so rich with history and spiritual references that it serves, in my mind, as the model for black visual biography and memoir.

From the onset of the film, Lemmons shows that Harriet's primary obsession is with God or, in Ifá, Oludumare. Her every concern is whether or not her actions, her decisions, her plans please an omnipotent, all-loving Creator. She talks to and consults Oludumare as if He is her very consciousness. I use the name Oludumare here because Harriet does not conceptualize God in the Christian sense; she understands God as a Yoruban might, summoning and meeting God not in an edifice but in the middle of the forest. She sees God as the Keeper of the universe and thus moves through the woods with quiet resolve because she believes Oludumare shields and protects her. This obeisance to Oludumare is the first requirement of an Ifá initiate.

Harriet acknowledges His omnipresence and authority and indeed elicits His wisdom as she completes her journeys. She searches constantly for Oludumare's signs—waving trees, still air, a disturbed consciousness—as they keep her from the snares of slave catchers. She also performs the ritual of "stilling" herself continuously in order to hear Oludumare's instructions. That she doesn't use the word "Oludumare" for God simply exposes that Africans were robbed of their native tongue during the journey across the seas. However, the absence of their language does not equal the absence of their African spiritual consciousness. Enslaved Africans simply translated words and ideas about God into English. So "Heavenly Father" is merely the English version of "Oludumare"—even when Africans themselves are unaware. Harriet acknowledges that she comes from people who walk with and know God intimately, and in that tradition, she moves and has her being. By the end of the movie, viewers see that everything Harriet does is the manifestation of spiritual consultation. The cornerstone of her many successful trips to freedom land is her unwavering belief in and coexistence with Oludumare, the Almighty God, who assures that no danger or evil will befall her.

The day she decides to run, she meets the Ifá river goddess, Oshun. Gideon, her former owner, traps her on a bridge, and

Harriet plunges straight into the rushing arms of this deity of love and beauty. One might assume it impossible to survive such a fall, but viewers soon learn that Oshun delivers Harriet in calmer waters downstream. Thus begins Harriet's lifelong relationship with streams, rivers, and bodies of moving water. This connection saves her and others countless times throughout her journeys. At one point, she and a band of fugitives are forced to a deep stream, which even Harriet is cautious of crossing. Yet having no other choice, Harriet enters the frigid water, trusting only that Oshun will usher them safely across. She leads the way, whispering intensely, "Rivers of living water, flow through me," and soon she and the runaways stand shivering but delivered on dry ground. No one knows how many rivers Harriet crossed in her day, but obviously she crossed them successfully. The movie implies that something in the water, some spiritual force, might've assisted her. Ifá practitioners call this power Oshun.

Later in the movie, Harriet sings Oshun's song in order to summon her power. She murmurs softly, loving, "Wade in the water, wade in the water, children. Wade in the water. God's gonna trouble the water." Then, troubled waters dissolve her scent and support her passage when land cannot help her. Often, even when she doesn't enter, she runs alongside streams and brooks as if Oshun is holding her hand. She needs Oshun in another sense, too, for Harriet is young and in love, and Oshun governs love and pleasure, standing guard over one's sensual desires. Harriet leaves her free husband, John, behind when she first escapes, hoping not to jeopardize his freedom. Yet when she returns for him, he has remarried, having assumed Harriet's death. Harriet is devastated, of course, and her heartbreak is a reality only Oshun can heal. Harriet soon discerns that her love for John was simply God's way of forcing her to return for her people. Now she knows what any Ifá initiate knows: that true love is oneness with Oludumare, a person's discovery of why he or she was sent. This recognition bespeaks Harriet's emotional maturity as well as her spiritual clarity that the loss of her husband cannot equal the loss of her people—a healing realization that only Oshun could've propagated.

Through the wisdom of her father, Harriet employs the strength of Obatala. Cloaked in white, Obatala is the father of Ifá deities, the keeper of virtue and moral integrity, the one who stands guard over the spirit of the others. Harriet's father, Ben, performs this exact function, and can be understood as the very manifestation of Obatala. When she is prepared to escape, he, cloaked in white, gives her a carved, wooden image of himself, a kind of talisman, to protect her along her way. Interestingly enough, the miniature statue is prepared *before* she runs, implying that her father has anticipated her mission. Likewise, Obatala is all-knowing, all-seeing, and interested most in the achievement of righteousness. Similarly, Ben covers his eyes when Harriet seeks his blessing and direction: he foresees slave catchers asking whether he has seen his daughter, and, not wanting to lie, he blindfolds himself and "sees" her, instead, with his heart. In other words, he intends to maintain good character, regardless of his circumstances. He believes in the virtue of his own spirit and refuses to compromise it—even in the midst of a diabolical slave system. The brilliance of this moment is that Kasi Lemmons demonstrates the small, yet transformative, ways in which enslaved Africans constructed and maintained their own personal agency. Plus, Ben is a free man. Yet he, like Obatala, governs the well-being of his children, so he will not escape north without them.

Whenever Harriet struggles, she reaches into her pocket and embraces her father, Obatala, who reminds her that nothing can destroy her if she believes in herself. This is ancestral reverence in action. This is Ifá made perfect.

Harriet soon discovers that her father, Obatala personified, knows things she does not know. When she decides to run, he sends her to Reverend Green for direction. Harriet understands Reverend Green as a sellout—a man who preaches only what white folks want to hear. His sermons are filled with scriptures of black subjugation, such as "slaves obey your masters." No one believes he is committed to the cause of liberty. However, Harriet discovers that Reverend Green is not what he seems. Indeed, he is a clandestine member of the Underground Railroad who tells her how to navigate her way north. Now she understands that her father, Ben, who has appeared blind, actually sees all things—an Obatala trait—and provides the direction for her destiny. As Obatala, Ben also knows the capacity of people's hearts—what they can carry, what might destroy them. So he sifts information about Harriet to his emotionally fragile wife. This saves her from unimaginable burdens and assists her survival as Harriet frees her siblings and prepares a home for them in the land of freedom.

Yet her mother, though mentally and emotionally limited, is spiritual too. Harriet's maternal inheritance is intangible, invisible, but no less formidable. Her birth name is Araminta, yet when she steps into freedom, she claims her mother's name: "Harriet," she tells William Still, boldly. "Name's Harriet." This declaration conjures her mother's coverage and courage as she runs. In Ifá terms, her mother, draped in blue, is Yemaya—the Great Mother, the Principle Nurturer, the Mighty Defender of Children. When she assumes her mother's name, she, by extension, becomes Yemaya in the flesh, the embodiment of communal motherhood and familial justice. She is the maternal instinct who sacrifices for her children, regardless of the cost. Harriet's transmutation into Yemaya explains her willingness to *force* some enslaved individuals into freedom, for her love is too wide, too deep, to leave them behind. They will either be free or die. This is her conviction, her life's mantra. This is a mother's unconditional love. This is the essence of Yemaya's embrace.

Of course Tubman needs all the protection she can get. Her life is fraught with trouble; by necessity, it must be. Her mission is the dismantling of a slave system that made white nations, including America, the financial envy of the world. They would not concede their human capital easily. America's hunger for Harriet's capture and destruction is palpable throughout this film. The bounty on her head is said to have been $40,000—an exorbitant amount in the mid-nineteenth century. Consequently, many sought her arrest. The movie depicts a black man, Bigger Long, who happily accepts the challenge of catching and returning her, although he, like everyone else, fails. Her previous owner, Gideon, also races for her apprehension and loses. Gideon is the white manifestation of Ajogun. He chases Harriet for the entirety of the film, and just when Bigger Long is about to kill her, he kills Bigger Long—solely for the right to destroy Harriet himself. He is white, but both forces are evil. They embody Ajogun or the forces of wickedness. These energies, which come in various representations, seek nothing but death, disease, and destruction, and their sole purpose is the fulfillment of humanity's malevolent desires.

That this energy is represented by both white and black men reflects the Ifá belief that wickedness knows no color, no human exceptions. Practically every slave insurrection, for example, was foiled by some desperate black soul who believed his or her loyalty to whiteness would pay off. It never did; it never does.

In the end, neither man will boast her destruction, for Harriet's spiritual stealth and righteousness undergird her subversion. This mutual desire to undermine Harriet's plan is the masterwork of Ajogun. It is the fruit of greed and capitalism, which drives a nation to destroy its citizens in exchange for their priceless labor. Consequently, when Harriet gets the opportunity to destroy Gideon, she doesn't. In fact, she won't. She knows firsthand the impact of evil on the human heart. She will not allow Ajogun residence in hers. Instead, she lowers the pointed gun and tells Gideon, "People ain't spose to own people," and rides off on his white horse. She chooses the sanctity of her spirit over the sinister pleasure of another's destruction, and thus preserves her allegiance to Oludumare and the precepts of Ifá.

Esu-Elegba, or the Great Trickster, also makes a cameo appearance in this film. Esu represents uncertainty, stealth, deceit, cunning, language interpretation, and destiny. Esu also sits at the crossroads of life—the intersection of possibilities—where life and death decisions are made. That's where viewers find Walter, the young man with the raccoon-tailed hat. He studies Harriet's ways, her geographical knowledge, and thus hopes to reap some of the reward of her capture. At one point, he lingers in a tree, just above Harriet's head, when she and a band of fugitives are fleeing slave catchers. Walter, embodying the spirit of Esu, has in fact followed her for miles, marking her twists and turns, reporting this navigation to bounty hunters just up the road. He thinks he has outwitted Harriet and is about to share in the spoils of her arrest, when, much to his surprise, Harriet falls to her knees in the midst of the forest and seeks Oludumare's divine guidance. Suddenly, she rises and makes an abrupt turn, shifting the band's direction. Walter is startled and amazed at Harriet's spiritual sensibilities, such that, unable to catch her, he soon approaches her and offers to support her cause. He says to Harriet, "You talks to God, and seem like God talks back to you." He pauses and continues sorrowfully: "I got some explaining [to God] to do." He becomes a reformed bounty hunter, functioning, for the remainder of the film, as Harriet's personal assistant. In other words, Walter's trickery and deceit were exposed and, in fact, transformed into good by Harriet's moral character. Tricks that were once meant for her capture become, in Esu's hands, the means of her escape. Whether a real-life Walter ever existed is immaterial; bounty hunters like him certainly did. Yet they did not win. Harriet's spiritual fortress protected her, even from invisible entities that might've enjoyed her demise.

Mentioned above, Reverend Green is the quintessential embodiment of Esu-Elegba. He is, from all appearances, the plantation's Uncle Tom who takes pride in reinforcing the slave system. Yet, as aforementioned, he is more than he appears. He conceals fugitives beneath the floor of the church, directly below the pulpit no less, and instructs Harriet on how to travel north on foot. He tells her to follow the stars, as a celestial map, and if it be cloudy, follow the river (Oshun). Then, in no uncertain terms, he looks directly into her eyes and declares, "Fear is your enemy." Harriet is stunned yet grateful. This is not the Reverend Green she knows. This is

Esu, the one who wears many masks and plays many subversive roles. He is the opposite of what she's assumed, assisting runaways while also providing, in the slave captor's hearing, the theological distraction necessary to assuage enemy eyes. Reverend Green is the double-tongued manipulator, recognizable only to those like Obatala (Harriet's father) who see both the visible and the invisible. Now Harriet knows that her survival depends upon Esu's instruction, so she becomes his most committed pupil.

Another Ifá deity, Osanyin, materializes in this film. As the keeper of forests and natural medicines, healing magic and spells, Osanyin hovers over Harriet as she runs and faints and hides in the dark forest. In fact, although Harriet experienced seizure-like fainting spells, which happened at arbitrary times, they never occurred midflight in the woods or at least never facilitated her capture. Followers of Ifá would say that, amidst the woodlands, Osanyin sheltered her. Indeed, Osanyin is honored every time she bows before a tree in search of Oludumare's wisdom. In Ifá epistemology, trees serve as the conduit or the keeper of spirit, and Harriet honors trees as she honors God. Osanyin resides in the trees, so as Harriet makes her offering to him, he covers and protects her as she moves.

Ogun, the warrior spirit, emerges in the person of Marie, the innkeeper and woman protectorate in Philadelphia. Although Ogun is generally masculine, Marie, like Ogun, is bold and courageous, the exemplary manifestation of African warrior essence. Ogun governs metals, tools, and weaponry, and as such Miss Marie gifts Harriet a gun then teaches her to use it. Even in the end, when faced with death, Marie's audacity never wavers. At gunpoint, she protects Harriet's mysterious whereabouts then dies a loyal soldier, a stalwart incarnation of Ogun's unrelenting spirit. The fact that Ogun is a woman here is Lemmons's brilliant way of disturbing patriarchal norms in black traditions and insisting that women are more than how they've been represented in the past. History doesn't tell the full story of the depth and sacrifice of black women and the roles they've played in the fight for their people's liberty. So Lemmons extends the narrative, freeing black women from stereotypical limitations and illustrating that many fought as valiantly as any man.

Harriet's story is known only because of a wise man named William Still, a real historical figure, who recorded it. And not only her story, but the testimony of hundreds of enslaved Africans who made their way to freedom with her help. This is the function of Orunmila, the writer of the text, the one who translates into print the desires of the gods for the people. In Ifá, Orunmila is the author of the Odu Ifá or the holy text—a combination of 256 verses that explain the ethical beliefs of Ifá practitioners. William Still plays this role in the narrative, constructing a living Odu for black Americans wherein escape narratives are recorded and thus preserved. This is critical—and historically accurate—because many, like Harriet, were illiterate and unable to write their own story. Hence, without this effort, she and so many others might've gone unknown. However, as Orunmila, William Still welcomes Harriet to Philadelphia and carefully records her amazing tale. He sits, like a great literary deity, with quill in hand, ready to document whatever she says. As incarnation of Orunmila, Still knows the power of the word and its importance to future generations. By capturing the details of her escape (and hundreds of others'), he has created a history, a counterhistory, for a people who had not yet been invited into American history. This is a spiritual process, to be sure, for the mere act of writing promises an empowered future, one which tells the truth of black people's struggle and unwavering determination. Actually, assuming the authority to construct one's own literary voice was as revolutionary as escape itself. So in the personhood of Orunmila, William Still transfers experience to text and thus constructs a document that will later prove that black people *always* resisted enslavement. This act further assures that nineteenth-century black voices never go unheard and that the price of freedom is never forgotten.

Kasi Lemmons is astute in her choice to centralize the power of literacy, given the state of education for black youth today. The precarious miseducation of black and brown children in American public schools has perpetuated the erroneous notion that writing is a European invention and, consequently, tangential to the legacy of black and brown cultures. Few schools teach that antebellum black writing was, in fact, an extension of the West African literary tradition, a practice which, on American plantations, was understood as insurrectionary—criminal even—far more dangerous and, as such, more influential than conventional weapons of warfare. Understood this way, black writing, then, becomes an act of war, a means by which the disinherited fight for and construct their own sovereignty. Without this knowledge, this Orunmila intentionality, black people could've been known as passive observers of time, those who accepted fate without resistance and wielded no assault against their oppression. This simply was not true. In fact, during enslavement, writing became the keeper of black integrity, the literary repository of black character and triumphant achievements. An African proverb says, "Until the gazelle tells the story, the lion will always be the victor."

This Harriet biopic celebrates black victory and guarantees the recognition of black cultural luminaries on their own terms. In truth, Kasi Lemmons is the real Orunmila, transferring to screen the story of a hero, our shero, who loved us enough to "prepare a place for us" in freedom. Lemmons takes creative license to ensure that we understand Harriet not merely as a historical figure, but also a mother, a goddess, who gave her life for her children. This movie, then, is a retelling of a biographical narrative in terms both historical and mythological. The truth lies nestled somewhere between.

At one point in the film, abolitionists gather in Philadelphia to discuss covert matters concerning the Underground Railroad. It is here that William Still announces that "only the initiated" can know and understand the contents of their meetings. Not many will understand this ancient spiritual referent; thus, key elements of this movie could easily be missed. Put simply, an initiate is one who seeks the meanings of life's mysteries. This person apprentices with a spiritual elder who teaches the importance of the seen and the unseen. Initiation moves someone from the mundane facets of life to the more complicated, less knowable realms of being. This is precisely the aim of Ifá—to usher people into a relationship with Oludumare and attendant orisha in order that they might know the full complexities of the human spirit. Harriet is obviously an initiate. She talks to God via trees; she follows the rhythm of the forest; she listens to the wind and waves. She survives countless trips across hostile terrain because the Invisible Ones guard and guide her. Northern abolitionists know this and thus welcome her, this self-made orisha, into the fold of the Keepers of Freedom. They now depend upon her, Mother Moses, the living Yemaya, to deliver others to free soil.

If one finds these orisha parallels merely coincidental, or even untenable, one should remember that, in the African worldview, the ubiquitous nature of spirit often comes unannounced. In fact, if one believes that Kasi Lemmons couldn't possibly have intended such parallels, I maintain that her conscious intention is irrelevant (although I believe in it). The spirit of Ifá governs this film, and the result is a visual spirituality, a graphic black ethos, that has the power to transform black viewers' self-perception.

Ultimately, Kasi Lemmons is our directorial Babalawo—the person in Ifá who reads signs and interprets divinations. Of course Babalawos are traditionally men, but Lemmons, once again, disrupts gender stratifications and becomes the *trans*gender ancestral authority who possesses the power and insight to conceptualize then visualize the totality of Harriet's multifaceted life. This metamorphosis is both part of Harriet's existence and of Lemmons's magic in telling the shero's tale. Lemmons assumes cultural and spiritual authority where women have not always been welcomed, and thus both tells and *creates* Harriet's story in ways that allow viewers to know her—not just know about her. Some truth is historical; some lingers in the spirit. This is the dichotomous reality of the black diaspora. If ever we find a storyteller who can traverse both domains, he or she can access our purest truth and illustrate the beauty and terror, the joy and immeasurable suffering of black life. Such is the person of Kasi Lemmons. She combines a historical Harriet with the Ifá spirit within her. Now we know why she—*and we*—survived.

THE POWER OF *POSE*

Most Americans in the 1980s and '90s had not yet decided queer people were people. Black and brown ones had a particularly difficult time, fighting racism and homophobia both at home and in the streets. Many were kicked out of families and churches, mocked in schools and other social institutions such that they were often left alone to die. Yet they didn't die. Some saved pennies and made their way to New York City where, together, they created living communities that sustained them against the odds. They were gay, lesbian, bisexual, trans, and searching for personal identities that were more complicated than most understood. What they had in common was the pain of rejection. But that didn't matter. They had learned early in life that, if they were going to live, they'd have to do so against the odds. And that's what they did. *POSE* illustrates the vicissitudes of daily life among fragile though brilliant LGBTQ souls who, during the AIDS epidemic, defied mainstream denunciation and, somehow, prospered.

I'm afraid many Americans might've missed the historical significance of *POSE*. I say this because, as I watched each episode with friends, some of them shrugged and declared the show simply "all right" and "okay." Critics, like James

Poniewozik of the *New York Times*, agreed. In his lukewarm appraisal, he says, "It is not flawless, but it defines its own category." I don't think they understood the price these black and brown queer bodies paid to fight death daily. My friends couldn't have comprehended the weight of having been dismissed and erased by the world while simultaneously struggling for value and meaning within it. If so, they might've cheered for these heros and sheros like I did. And clearly they didn't understand the emotional cost of having been cast away by family, only to spend a lifetime searching for the closest substitute they could find. I've never seen such strength, such bold resolve, such determination to be something other than what society says you are. These queer young people are the twentieth-century warriors of freedom. Somehow, they rewrote history as they lived it, constructing for themselves lives of significance and merit while combating the public's declaration of their uselessness. I shook my head after every episode, wondering how in the world they survived when the entirety of America, it seemed, was against them. By the end of the series, I knew: they gathered resources and created matrices of healing that protected them from the storm of homophobia and trans hatred, which most citizens undoubtedly hoped would silence them forever.

Yet these daring, defiant, brave spirits didn't simply survive; they crafted the creative expressions that shaped the aesthetics of '80s popular culture. Lesbian girls and gay boys, trans men and women, displayed gifts and talents too magnificent to be ignored. They weren't willing to hide away for the world's comfort. Quite the antithesis, they took matters into their own hands and made a world so original, so dazzlingly beautiful, that the larger society had no choice but to take notice. They created ballroom performances, which featured fashions and dance styles that set trends for decades. The voguing phenomenon, for instance, which Madonna borrowed and pimped, was birthed and perfected in gay ballrooms. No one could outperform "the children" when it came to creative nuances of this dance, and major artists like Michael Jackson borrowed influences from these underground virtuosos. Some heteronormatives belittled them as "freaks," but once their creativity burst forth, naysayers fell silent. Artistic credit came years later, but Ballroom revealed to the world the creative value of those who had been muzzled and demeaned. The series illustrates beautifully the hard work and masterful details that went into these midnight performances, proving that they were more than children playing dress-up. Actually, they were a desperate attempt by a rejected population to make their divine presence known.

I am consistently flabbergasted at the magic, mystery, and delight of Ballroom culture. These children—poor, often uneducated, and consumed with hurt and grief—turn makeup, high heels, and evening gowns into garments that sparkle and astound even a sneering public. Their boldness mirrors that of fearless soldiers—for the ballroom runway isn't for the faint of heart. If yo shit ain't correct, laid, and snatched, you will be humiliated beyond repair. In essence, the Ballroom is black excellence in fashion and personal imagination. There is no room for mediocrity since performances are the last-ditch effort of an excluded population to present their social significance before the world's contemptuous eyes. Said differently, the glam and glitter of gay Ballroom culture functioned to expose the depth of brilliance, creativity, and innovation that only "the children" could deliver. In their behavior, they said,

"We might go to Hell, but, baby, Hell will never be the same when we get there!"

To be sure, these children transmute and synthesize pain into performance. This is the black survival ethic made perfect. Transforming hog guts into a delicacy called chitlins is the same trick as refashioning trauma into a sparkling sequined dress. No one expected these kids—or any of their ancestors on slave ships—to do anything but die. Yet they wipe their tears and strut streets and alleys with damaged hearts until enough strength arrives that they don't need Momma and Daddy's affirmation anymore. They discover that true family is the people who *choose* to love you—not those who are supposed to.

However, the series is not perfect. Some of the acting is bad and a few stereotypes abound. But that doesn't subtract from the overall strength of the effort. In fact, what moves me is that, finally, LGBTQ history is part of the national narrative. Queer kids aren't a secret anymore. And although some of them die from AIDS in the series, that doesn't lessen their legacy. I know what many Americans thought of AIDS. They called it "the faggot's due." They said things like, "That's what they get!" and "You can't live in sin forever!" Those who didn't say this said nothing. I don't recall many mainstream figures or institutions lending their voices or influence to save the lives of black and brown gay kids. What I remember most is the critique of the church and the uncontested verbal abuse that, in the '80s, became part of American vernacular. People said "faggots" and "bulldaggers" from pulpits and street corners. Some music lyrics included these shameful words. Still, watching queer children fight and argue for their humanity made me proud. Few respected LGBTQ people during that time and fewer believed they'd been born this way. Many of the children didn't believe it either. Yet what they knew for sure was that they deserved God's breath. Watching them take it and use it to expand the nation's consciousness around gender and sexuality excited my soul.

That's the transformative lesson of *POSE*: that oppressed people can and will construct their own reality when they learn to dream beyond others' imagination. And these kids dream big. Some want to be doctors and nurses; others, dancers and runway models. But what they all want is to be different and unashamed. They are not willing to trade personal identities simply to be accepted by the mainstream. In fact, they are willing to struggle in poverty before they compromise themselves for jobs and/or public applause. I've rarely been so gratified. These young people manifest humanity's best self. Some of them stand with character and pay bills for relatives who humiliate them a lifetime. King would be pleased, I thought. But then I recalled his silence around Bayard Rustin and, once again, shook my head.

I was an undeclared fluid teen in the '80s, and I remember painfully the beatings and cursing so many gay children received as the price of their truth. Some parents' abuse sent children to the hospital. Others put them out in the rain and snow. I remember holding hands and crying with friends because they had no place to go. Some withdrew into silence and depression. Others were too different to hide. That's what infuriated parents—when a child's difference embarrassed the family, when their truth was too obvious to lie about. And most parents were certainly willing to lie. No one wanted *that* in the family. So those who couldn't mask their identity paid hell for it. They were called despicable names—sissy, punk, butch, faggot, bulldagger—and often beaten without apology. I wondered why God didn't intervene. God didn't agree, did He? That's why so many young queers left the church—because God was as silent and inactive as most Americans. And what kind of God would let others treat His children this way? We were children of God, too, weren't we?

That's what this show is about—the ways in which deserted children demand space in American society. Elektra Abundance, for instance, endures humiliation from mainstream culture while using her body to make a living, since most businesses wouldn't hire trans people. Blanca, her daughter, starts her own house and shelters kids the way her mother does, believing that, as long as they stay together, they will prosper. Blanca becomes a nurse and sends one of her sons to dance school, an unbelievable achievement from one who starts with nothing. The emcee of the ballroom, Pray Tell, gives his precious new HIV medicine to a younger lover, thereby paying the ultimate price—his own life—for the boy's continued existence. These characters—and their real-life representatives—paid enormously to be seen and respected. Their being cost them everything, and, against the odds, they paid it, thus creating worth and significance from lives once thought meaningless. In many ways, *POSE* is an elegy to the AIDS generation, an obeisance to the burgeoning gay community it sustained. Again, I lived through that era, and I saw the battle people waged simply to justify their lives. But *POSE* exposed that something magical happened back then, something supernatural that probably took God's breath away: LGBTQ youth insisted upon their humanity, whether the world agreed or not. And by being human they became divine—made in the image of God like everyone else.

I admire most the way these black and brown children refuse their intended captivity. Like their white queer peers across America at the time, they are familial castoffs who find their way to New York City, hoping that, somehow, against the popular narrative, they can discover a place where they aren't castigated for their difference. As aforementioned, while there, these queer kids create community and thus defy what the world thinks about them. They become mothers and fathers, sisters and brothers, and move into "houses" that protect them from a cruel, insensitive world. These "mothers" are often transgender women who extend loving arms around naive kids who, otherwise, would have no protective fortress at all. Because of the genius of these oppressed souls, they fashion a way of life that allows them to thrive when many counted them among the dead. They huddle together in shanty apartments where they share meals, dreams, and lives unknown to the general public. Behind closed doors, these resolute LGBTQ souls share contracts of intimacy that last a lifetime. Their survival demonstrates that they mean to change the world—not succumb to it. And they do. They are battered and disgraced, but such treatment only fuels their determination to succeed. The brilliance of *POSE* is that it shows how resilient souls fought against a zero-sum image and constructed for themselves a world, a life, when most Americans had decided there was no use for them.

The sad thing about the series is the sheer number of people who died alone from AIDS. This is why the black gay community was and is so powerful and valuable—it was the last stronghold most of them had, their only comfort when HIV swallowed so many whole. As you watch the series, you get a sense of how precious early HIV medicine was and how its distribution was class and race stratified. More specifically, the series shows how black and Latino HIV carriers like Pray Tell and Blanca were often excluded from medical trials and experiments that were the best hope for life during those years. Few public officials cared much about the AIDS epidemic, and thus poor, disenfranchised, uninsured queers trembled in hospital beds and on ragged floor mattresses while doctors and medical staff pretty much ignored them. On their own, they fought an invisible battle they were foretold to lose. Some won, but far too many lost, so they marched to funeral after funeral, burying talent and genius so rare only God knows who we truly lost during those years. At the height of the epidemic, the public message was clear: death is the reward of the unrepentant queer. This missive caused many to drown in drug use as they tried to digest the truth of their unwelcomed identity. Still, most didn't go down without a fight. They covered boils with foundation and stomped to the club and walked—until they couldn't.

No one knows the pain of losing friends every day like survivors of the '80s AIDS crisis. And "every day" is no exaggeration. Sometimes, precious gay souls were left in funeral parlors with no biological family to claim them. Some were buried in unmarked graves with no headstone at all. When there wasn't enough money to bury them, their emaciated bodies were cremated and never mentioned again. Several were laid to rest with no ritual to commemorate their existence—as if the world wanted no memory of them. Friends gathered privately and wept for those they knew. As shown in *POSE*, the world seemed to want their obliteration, their literal eradication from the earth. Some doctors and nurses, like Blanca, sympathized with sufferers of AIDS and committed their lives to nurturing patients and supporting their dignity as they weakened. But many others shunned them and dismantled their self-worth by providing minimal care and verbal reprimands like "shoulda used a condom." The horror stories of how medical officials handled AIDS patients would make anyone tremble these days, but such neglect and abuse were common in the '80s, buttressed with the belief that AIDS was the corrective to a wanton population of sexual degenerates. Billy Porter, as Pray Tell, demonstrates brilliantly the emotional and psychological impact these daily deaths had on those left behind, and how, often, the resulting trauma made HIV survivors hate that they had survived. He is one of the series' shining moments, living truth boldly and flaunting clothes and confidence as if having descended from royalty. Once he contracts HIV, he returns home to confront demons and relatives who once considered him nothing but a church sissy. Then, after laying them to rest, he returns to New York and teaches youngsters in the Ballroom community how to die with dignity. His private fears and sorrows are displayed sensitively, demonstrating the complexities of his humanity, but ultimately Pray Tell is deified as the Grand Emcee of the LGBTQ nation. His influence shields the others like angels' wings, protecting a group of people who will one day get their moment in the sun. But for now, he dies, like so many others of the era, having come before most could see his glory.

Another transformative feature of *POSE* is the unbelievable sense of community these kids establish. They collect dollars and save each other from destructive decisions that could've ruined them forever. They share clothes and resources in order to support each other's dreams. Like in any other community, they fight and betray, but they also forgive and sacrifice, sometimes with cash and sometimes with their mere presence. They even hold each other accountable to healthy behavior, although they avoid judgment since their very existence is considered a social deviation. As aforementioned, many depend on sex work for their living, but this does not deteriorate their integrity. Rather, in some instances, it upholds it, for it reinforces desirability where only worthlessness once dwelled. They give their very lives to assure the future of their community. They even cover each other's personal and legal indiscretions. This is tribal identity among the despised and detested. This is also an announcement to the world that the denied stone will not be denied forever. These families and communities love and struggle, laugh and die, like all families, but their existence shows that human beings will make a community if they're not invited into one.

I should point out that contemporary gender and sex terminology so willingly used by scholars today was rooted in the attempt of '80s sexual rejects to find or create language that reflects the beauty of their existence. American culture now speaks of trans people instead of "weirdos" and knows to avoid pejorative terms like "dykes" and "faggots" because a whole generation marched and fought to be seen and understood as humans—not freaks. Terms such as "non-binary" and "fluid" are now part of the American lexicon due, in part, to the work of black queerfolk like Jewelle Gomez, Barbara Smith, Anita Cornwell, Audre Lorde, and Assotto Saint who stood on the front lines of the gay movement when most black queers avoided the public eye. I love that *POSE* characters, who exist in a time before a mainstream understanding of transgender identity evolved, speak of each other as "different" and validate their transness with words we now use to embrace such truths. These are not children simply rebelling out of defiance; these are beings clearing the way for a soon-coming decade when everyone would catch up to the reality of their complexity and discover, finally, that gender and sexuality have always been ignored frontiers on the American landscape. Indeed, few politicians or scholars had much celebratory to say about them at the time. Yet because they stood their ground and produced art, literature, and philosophies too brilliant to dismiss, the country acknowledges their humanity today. Modern America's fight to regard the colored gay community as legitimate is precisely because many like Baldwin, Lorde, and Rustin shifted the intellectual discourse so intensely that they have to be acknowledged. If they were regular, ordinarily talented people, most of them and their community would still be unseen and unheard. This means, in essence, that if gay people can prove their value, they'll get invited into humanity. If their art mesmerizes and their writing compels and their dance hypnotizes and their music transforms, we'll respect them and make room for them at the table. Woe unto regular, everyday gay boys and girls who might have to remain faggots and dykes until they do something remarkable enough to be deemed human.

Many scholars have now written about and documented the power and complexity of '80s Ballroom culture: Marlon Bailey's *Butch Queens Up in Pumps*, Gerald Gaskin's *Legendary: Inside the House Ballroom Scene*, Chantal Regnault's *Voguing and the House Ballroom Scene of New York, 1989-92*, and *POSE* brings this scholarship to life. In 1990, the iconic movie *Paris Is Burning* hit the scene and exposed to the world the magic and creative mastery of these underground performances. Thereafter, queer lives became spectacle as the protective shield of silence and secrecy vanished away. *POSE* is a symbolic homage to the lives of those who fought the early battles in the war for gender and sexual equality, a war that only now has gained a modicum of respect. Many members of this maligned community sacrificed their very lives to exist authentically, thus preparing the way for contemporary LGBTQ offspring to declare their difference without shame or fear of retribution.

I think of activists like Marsha P. Johnson who fought for black queer rights long before anyone respected her black queer body. Indeed, no one knows the emotional turmoil she endured as others inquired about her genitalia and tried to force her into a biological inevitability that did not represent her truth. She and other social activists and house mothers then pimped this perceived ambiguity, selling their bodies in seedy nightclubs and dark alleys to fetish-seeking men who paid good money for an uncharacteristic sexual experience. Yet the use of their bodies was a high price to pay, for it often meant the contracting of venereal diseases and ultimately the spreading of HIV, which almost destroyed their entire community. Still, their motive reflected that of any teenager in the '80s and '90s—a longing for a taste of the American dream of wealth and material excess. That it often cost their lives was simply the price of the dream.

POSE exemplifies the resilience and durability of the human spirit. I fear that many Americans might have skipped this show, both because of the people it represents and their unconventional lifestyle. Yet the lessons of their existence transform stereotypes into spiritual insight. Their bodies bore the scars of a nation which, prior to the 2000s, had little room or tolerance for them. These determined spirits stood in the face of blatant opposition and taught America that part of its very strength lies in its LGBTQ population. In fact, the undeniable talent of this community raised the bar on the standard of public creative performances in the 1980s. Their unmatched genius, evidenced first by their physical eccentricity, bespeaks the freedom of an era of misfits who refused to be anything other than themselves. This freedom, I argue, was bequeathed to future generations by these young queer ones—those in the '80s who pranced about while being despised and disparaged. Their refusal to disappear morphed into power and economic strength America could not ignore. Now we bow before those who survived our ridicule and held fast to the belief that they, too, were children of God.

Forgive America, Lord, for ever having believed otherwise.

CLARK ATLANTA UNIVERSITY: HOME OF THE HOLY GHOST

A commencement speech delivered on May 18, 2024

HERE THEY COME, Y'ALL, HERE THEY COME!... HERE THEY COME, Y'ALL, HERE THEY COME!

Doctors, lawyers, writers, business owners, teachers, healers, rappers, preachers,

Here they come, y'all, here they come!

Psychologists, sociologists, anthropologists, zoologists, ethnomusicologists, paleontologists,

Here they come, y'all, here they come!

Anesthesiologists, cosmetologists, dermatologists, embryologists, ontologists, epidemiologists, ophthalmologists, radiologists, blackologists,

Here they come, y'all, here they come!

Computer scientists, mechanical engineers, nurses, architects, radio/TV/film producers, economists, accountants, marketing geniuses, chemists, business analysts,

Here they come, y'all here they come!

Musicians, mathematicians, astronauts, philosophers, pharmacists, dentists, historians, speech therapists, HR specialists, painters, dancers, actors, janitors, street sweepers, postal workers, plumbers, electricians, paramedics, bakers, construction workers, hairdressers, insurance agents, librarians, veterinarians, humanitarians,

Here they come, y'all, here they come! Here they come, y'all, here they come!

The dream of the slave, the hope of the angels, the promise of the ancestors, the answer to grandmama's prayers, the guarantee of granddaddy's work!

Here they come, y'all, here they come! Here they come, y'all, here they Come!

The cure for cancer is sitting right here! The antidote for sickle cell is sitting right here! The great negotiator of war and peace is about to get a degree! The community of billionaires is gathered right here!

Here they come, y'all, here they come! Here they come, y'all, here they come!

This is how you know the Holy Ghost lives here…because somebody doubted you, but here you are! Somebody said, "No Way" but the Holy Ghost said, "Hell yeah!"

For some of you, the ends didn't meet! The money didn't add up! You had to retake a class. You got discouraged, almost dropped out, got frustrated, but the Holy Ghost said, "Hell yeah!"

For some of you, you buried someone you loved along the way. You lost more than your heart could take. You cried in the midnight hour, and you told God, "I can't do this no more!" But the Holy Ghost said, "Hell yeah!"

For some of you, you worked twenty, sometimes thirty, hours a week, trying to keep yo phone on and a few groceries in the fridge, and you actually sent Momma a little money when you could. It got heavy, and you almost quit. You said, "I'm done. I just don't have it," but the Holy Ghost said, "Hell yeah!"

For some of you, you gave your heart to someone else and they didn't respect it. They took you as a plaything and toyed with your emotions. THEY thought they were special, but really you were the gift. Still, you were the one hurt and devastated in the end. They thought you were down for the count. But baby, they didn't know you! They're looking at you today, saying, "No way!" and the Holy Ghost is saying, "Hell Yeah!"

See, anywhere the Holy Ghost resides, there will be magic. There will be promise. There will be possibilities. And the Holy Ghost has come today to tell you that you didn't pay all this money to doubt yourself. You didn't pay all this money to wonder if you're good enough. You didn't pay all this money to be unsure of your beauty! You didn't pay all this money to wonder whether or not you'll get a job. You didn't pay all this money to sit on the sidelines and clap. No, ma'am, no, sir! You're the MVP now. That's right, it's you. LISTEN! If Harriett Tubman ran to freedom, you can run to your destiny! King didn't march for you to get a degree and chill. Bayard Rustin didn't organize so you could clap for him. Black folk didn't pick cotton so you could look cute in a black robe! Shirley Chisholm didn't run for president so you could run away from Adversity! Nat Turner didn't lead a slave rebellion so you could be afraid of your own voice! James Baldwin didn't write beautifully so you could simply praise his words! Fannie Lou Hamer didn't stand up so you could sit down! George T. French Jr. didn't come to CAU because he had nowhere else to go! The faculty doesn't teach here because we wonder whether we'll see black students graduate.

We teach here because black excellence is our hobby, it's our daily bread, our living water, our reason for waking up in the morning. We teach here because every day we come to work, WE SEE GOD: We see God chillin on the promenade, We see God stepping in Greek paraphernalia, We see God rushing to hand in a late paper, We see God shouting to a homey across the way! We see God slinging braids to the right and the left and strutting like she knows who the hell she is! We see God struttin out of Carl Mary Ware with the freshest fade in the AUC and sneakers so white they glow in the dark! We see God with locks, and wigs, and weaves, and extensions, in every shade of black conceivable. One day, God is caramel mocha, another day God is peanut-butter brown, another day God is burnt russet, another day God is deep dark chocolate, another day God is golden honey brown, another day God is shiny black onyx, another day God is chestnut, another day God is beige, another day God is bronze, another day God is coffee with cream, another day God is mahogany fine, another day God is copper bisque, another day God is sweet cinnamon, another day God is almond butter...but every day God is black at CAU, showin us how to find a way or make one!

Don't you know that, four hundred years ago, they thought they had destroyed us? And that they owned us? They scattered us around the world, thinking they had destroyed us, but we kept on coming. That's what we do! We keep on coming! We are the keepa-coming people! Like...[students' names]. We are the seeds of Africa, we are hope manifested! But the dumbest thing slavers ever did was to scatter seeds around the world. Because if you want to destroy seed, you don't scatter it. Scattered seeds bloom and blossom everywhere you throw them! Any piece of soil they can grab, they hold on to for dear life and come forth against the odds. We are the keepa-coming people. Folks keep putting stumbling blocks in our way, without knowing that we turn stumbling blocks into stepping stones and rise higher every time. These folks don't know who the hell they brought here! They don't know who the hell they enslaved! They thought they brought Negroes to America! They didn't know they brought healers and weavers and cooks and farmers and spiritualists and inspirers and teachers and philosophers and psychologists and drummers to this land! They brought dancers and poets and fashion divas and writers and athletes and singers and entrepreneurs and painters and sculptors. They thought that because we were naked, they had striped Africa from us. But they didn't know that Africa ain't ON you; Africa is IN you! And everything we were, we still are. Listen, You are in the lineage of the great musician Fletcher Henderson, who graduated from this fabulous university in 1920. You are in the lineage of Mary Frances Early and Marva Collins, creator of the world-renowned Westside Preparatory School in Chicago, which transformed the lives of poor black geniuses in the 1970s and '80s. You are in the lineage of brilliant minds like Kenny Leon and Kenya Barris. You are in the lineage of genius entrepreneurs like Pinky Cole and Harry Pace. Who is Harry Pace, you ask? He was the founder of Black Swan Records—the first black-owned record label during the Harlem Renaissance. He graduated valedictorian from Atlanta University in 1903. He was only nineteen years old. Baby, that's black genius! That's the legacy of Clark Atlanta University! And you're also in the lineage of Dr. Daniel Black, who, at eighteen, entered Clark College in 1984 and graduated four years later, magna cum laude. Dr. Black went on to earn degrees from Oxford University, Oxford, and a

PhD from Temple University's first-ever African American Studies program. Dr. Black is the author of several bestselling books, namely, *They Tell Me of a Home*, *Perfect Peace*, *The Coming*, *Don't Cry for Me*, *Black on Black*, and soon to be released, a black scripture, a new BLACK Bible titled *The Good Book*. You got to know where you come from, you got to know who you with, you got to know who you been taught by! You got to know who you rubbin shoulders with! Don't waste your time comparing yourself to other people when you're surrounded by God's holy angels.

There are other schools around,
But they not like us
Good schools, great schools,
But they not like us
This is CAU! The proud, the few,
The place where excellence debuts!
They not like us!

You say you need a degree?
Well, we confer three—
The bachelors, the master's, and the PhD
They not like us!

If you want some knowledge,
Don't just go to a college,
Get to CAU, where ignorance is taboo
They not like us!

It's truly divine,
When two institutions combine
And become home to the divine nine

But don't be confused,
We step, and party till bemused
They not like us

Your job is to lift us high!
Far, far into the sky
This ain't no trick!
We gotta do better than Drake AND Kendrick!

We standin on business!

This the home of the Holy Ghost,
The last and the foremost,
The East and the West Coast,
God's mighty guidepost,
The potatoes and the rump roast,
The coffee and the black toast!

If you need Heaven in your view,
Get yoself to CAU!

These people don't know you! They don't think you're gonna be a lawyer, but you are! They don't think you're going get into med school, but you are! They don't know that you're going to teach in public school and change the way black children see themselves, but you are! They don't know that you're gonna open a new business no one has ever heard of, but you are! They think that just 'cause you came from a school they ain't never heard of that you ain't the one! But baby, listen! Most folks can't tell you where Jesus went to school, but they sho know His name! Just like they're about to know yours! And the Holy Ghost ain't gon let you lose! So when people doubt you, dance, graduates, dance! When people talk about you, dance, graduates, dance! When people laugh at you, dance, graduates, dance! When people don't believe in you, dance! When people think they got over on you, get the hell up and dance! When ain't no money on yo debit card, dance! When you gotta collect change to buy a little gas, dance! When you gotta wash some underwear by hand, dance! When yo phone is turned off, dance, black people, dance! When it looks like all hope is gone, dance, baby, dance, 'cause that's when the Holy Ghost is settin you up and gettin the world ready to meet and receive a black savior this time! You wanna boss up your life? All you gotta do is get in with me! and remember that there are other schools around, but they NOT LIKE US!